Enhancing Clinical Case Formulation

Clinical formulation lies at the heart of how mental health professionals understand psychological distress. It is the application of a framework that cohesively integrates scientific knowledge with the symptoms of distress. In essence, it is the creation of order to what is often experienced as disorder. The aim of this book is to bring awareness to the theoretical and practical opportunities for mental health professionals that exist by using atypical information when adapting typical formulation models.

Each chapter reflects some variation in how formulation is defined, conceptualised, and practiced, by using information that regularly materializes from professional encounters but often is omitted from the formulation of a particular presenting problem. Chapters on diet and exercise, sleep, spirituality, sexuality and meaning-making highlight how approaches to formulation can be extended to provide additional opportunities for intervention for the client and practitioner.

A professional encounter orientated in the manner proposed will generate a type of formulation that will raise interesting and testable hypotheses that can assist in understanding 'stuck' points in therapy, difficulties within the therapeutic relationship, low motivation or inability to engage in particular approaches and will assist in devising person-specific mental health interventions. This book will appeal to clinical psychologists and psychotherapists in practice and training.

Patrick Ryan has worked as a clinical psychologist for 23 years. He is the Director of Clinical Psychology and Head of the Department of Psychology at the University of Limerick, Ireland. A clinical practitioner, he remains involved in clinical training, research, supervision and mental health consultancy.

'This book is a gem. It is both thoughtful and practical. It challenges mental health professionals to use the formulation process to understand people, rather than just their problems. The central idea is to promote recovery by taking a wide-angle perspective on the complexities of clients' whole lives rather than zeroing in on their specific difficulties. There is a refreshing invitation to consider neuroscience, meaning-making, personality, sexuality, spirituality, nutrition, physical exercise, sleep and other variables in the formulation process. This book will be of interest to both mental health professionals in training and experienced clinicians.' — **Alan Carr**, PhD, Professor of Clinical Psychology, University College Dublin, Ireland

'This book represents a much-welcomed addition to the literature on formulation in clinical practice. Unlike other texts, it promotes formulation as an attempt to consider the whole person in contrast to predominantly being concerned with problems and deficits. It is suggested that we need to start formulation by including a focus on clients' interests, strengths and competencies. This approach invites clinicians to work collaboratively alongside clients in a way that encourages generating positive, solution-oriented formulations. This also opens the door to formulation as a part of early intervention to generate hope and suggest resources that can be employed to the advantage of clients and clinicians.' — **Rudi Dallos**, Professor and Research Director, Clinical Psychology, University of Plymouth, UK

Enhancing Clinical Case Formulation

Theoretical and Practical Approaches
for Mental Health Practitioners

Edited by
Patrick Ryan

Routledge
Taylor & Francis Group

LONDON AND NEW YORK

First published 2020
by Routledge
2 Park Square, Milton Park, Abingdon, Oxon OX14 4RN

and by Routledge
52 Vanderbilt Avenue, New York, NY 10017

Routledge is an imprint of the Taylor & Francis Group, an informa business

© 2020 selection and editorial matter, Patrick Ryan; individual chapters, the contributors

The right of Patrick Ryan to be identified as the author of the editorial material, and of the authors for their individual chapters, has been asserted in accordance with sections 77 and 78 of the Copyright, Designs and Patents Act 1988.

All rights reserved. No part of this book may be reprinted or reproduced or utilised in any form or by any electronic, mechanical, or other means, now known or hereafter invented, including photocopying and recording, or in any information storage or retrieval system, without permission in writing from the publishers.

Trademark notice: Product or corporate names may be trademarks or registered trademarks, and are used only for identification and explanation without intent to infringe.

British Library Cataloguing-in-Publication Data
A catalogue record for this book is available from the British Library

Library of Congress Cataloging-in-Publication Data
A catalog record has been requested for this book

ISBN: 978-1-138-59832-4 (hbk)
ISBN: 978-1-138-59834-8 (pbk)
ISBN: 978-0-429-48641-8 (ebk)

Typeset in Times New Roman
by Nova Techset Private Limited, Bengaluru & Chennai, India

For Jed

Thinker, theorist, talker – always remembered

Contents

Contributors

Emma Breen, BA Psychology; MSc Applied Psychology; PhD (Clinical Psychology), is a clinical psychologist with Enable Ireland, Early Childhood Services, Meath, Ireland.

Kristina Cahill, BSc Psychology; MSc Abormal & Clinical Psychology; PhD (Clinical Psychology), is a clinical psychologist in the Adult Primary Care Psychology Service, Health Services Executive, Wicklow, Ireland.

Rory Carolan, BA Psychology; MSc Applied Psychology; PhD (Clinical Psychology), works as a clinical psychologist in Our Lady's Children's Hospital, Crumlin, Dublin, Ireland.

Fergal Connolly, BA Psychology; MSc Clinical Psychology & Health Services, works as an assistant psychologist at St James' Hospital, Dublin, Ireland, and as a research associate at the University of Limerick, Ireland.

Mary Kelly, BSc Psychology at the National University of Ireland, Galway; MSc Occupational Therapy; PhD (Clinical Psychology) at the University of Limerick, Ireland; works as a Clinical Psychologist in a lifespan Primary Care based in Kildare, Ireland.

Marie Kennedy, BSc Psychology; MSc Applied Psychology; PhD (Clinical Psychology), works as a clinical psychologist in a Child and Family Clinical Psychology Service, in the Health Services Executive, Limerick, Ireland.

Aoife Kilroe, BA; HDip (Psych); MSc; PhD (Clinical Psychology), works as a clinical psychologist in a Primary Care, Child, Adolescent and Family Service, in the Health Services Executive, Cork, Ireland.

Julie Lynch, BSc; MSc Applied Psychology, works as a psychologist in the Department of Psycho-Oncology at St Vincent's University Hospital, Dublin. She is currently engaged in clinical psychology doctoral education at University College Dublin, Ireland.

Dermot McMahon, BSc Psychology (Hons); MSc Applied Psychology; PhD (Clinical Psychology), works as a clinical psychologist in Adult Mental Health Services in the Health Services Executive, Cork/Kerry Community Mental Health Services, Ireland.

Eve Pender, BA Psychology; MSc Applied Psychology, in Mental Health; PhD (Clinical Psychology), works as a clinical psychologist with KARE, a voluntary sector service for people with intellectual disabilities, Kildare, Ireland.

Patrick Ryan, BA (Hons.) Psychology; DClinPsych, works as a clinical psychologist at the University of Limerick, Ireland, where he is the Head of the Department of Psychology. He is the Director of Clinical Psychology since 2005.

Eva Usher, BA Psychology & Sociology; H.Dip. Psychology; H.Dip.lay Therapy; MA Play Therapy; MSc Applied Psychology, is currently completing her PhD in Clinical Psychology at the University of Limerick, Ireland.

Research and technical support

Caitlyn Jensen works as a research associate in the Department of Psychology at the University of Limerick, Ireland.

Preface

The concept for 'Enhancing Formulation' emerged originally from my frustration in having to deal with seemingly insurmountable amounts information about clients that 'would not fit' with how I was supposed to conceptualise psychological distress. None of the best argued theoretical models, the sharpest formulation frameworks, nor the clearest diagnostic methodologies seemed to capture and utilise information that I found meaningful, and useful, in understanding psychological distress. Yet, such information was emerging from therapeutic conversations that formed the substantive part of my practice, and this was often where clients exposed their greatest strengths and vulnerabilities.

This book is the tangible manifestation of that original clinical frustration, somewhat turned on its head. It is my attempt to probe and co-ordinate the intellectual talent of my clinical colleagues, now my co-authors, so that we could address this 'random data' and meaningfully engage with it, whilst holding the integrity of our best practice approaches and orientations.

My aim is to bring awareness to material that surrounds us in our everyday practice, that can assist more with 'understanding the person' and less with 'diagnosing the condition'. The book is not solely an antithesis to prevailing practice paradigms – it aims to complement these paradigms, where possible, amongst practitioners. It does not represent a new model, framework or theory; rather it seeks to bring added value to material that we have routine access to when we engage with our clients.

The chapters that follow present some of the many factors of human experience, that may offer an alternative lens through which distress can be viewed. These factors are of my choosing and make no claim as to exclusivity or hierarchy of importance for practitioners. Indeed the argument for the inclusion of other important influences would more than adequately meet an aim of the book to raise awareness of what practitioners can work with in clinical practice.

It is my wish that you might discuss, debate, and argue, for and against, what we have written, and in doing so, generate the type of energy that relieves frustration, enhances creativity and expands our understanding of psychological distress through comprehensive, meaningful and purposeful formulation.

Patrick Ryan

Acknowledgements

I wish to acknowledge our appreciation of the entire team at Routledge involved in the commissioning, editing and production processes for this book. Transforming the original concept into the final product is a result of dedicated, professional and supportive work. I have experienced that support from the outset, so to Joanne Forshaw and her entire team, I express my grateful thanks.

This book emerged from the context of the brilliantly dynamic Department of Psychology at the University of Limerick, Ireland. I wish to make explicit my appreciation of the team of academics, administrative & technical staff and practitioners that I work with daily, whose mission is to nurture creativity as well as productivity. Your contribution in creating a fantastic work environment is much appreciated and not taken for granted.

Finally, I wish to acknowledge and honour the life-stories of the clients with whom the authors have worked. These stories have assisted and challenged us as practitioners in how we think about mental health and mental distress, and helped to ensure that as well as being scientist-practitioners, we are perpetual students of life.

Chapter 1

Enhancing formulation

Patrick Ryan and Aoife Kilroe

The process of clinical formulation aims to provide a psychological understanding of a person's difficulties and generally act as a guide for the clinician towards a particular intervention plan to help address these difficulties (Brown and Völlm, 2013). Despite this core skill being considered the 'bread and butter' of mental health practitioners in the fields of psychology and psychotherapy, professionals often struggle to assimilate substantial quantities of information into a coherent framework. In addition, the varying emphases in different approaches necessarily give precedence to specific but disparate information from assessment practices.

In the cognitive behavioural approach, constructing a formulation focuses on presenting, precipitating, perpetuating, predisposing and protective factors (Dudley and Kuyken, 2014; Kuyken et al. 2009). The psychodynamic perspective targets the matrix of dynamic, developmental, structural and adaptive patterns in which individuals approach inner conflict (Leiper, 2014). The systemic perspective constructs a formulation based on interpersonal interactions between the individual and their wider systems, in particular, the family system (Dallos and Stedmon, 2014). Although each has its own merits and relevance for how to approach an individual case, each is also limited in terms of the boundaries they place on what type of information is incorporated into the formulation. Information that may be integral to understanding a person's difficulties (e.g. personality factors, spiritual belief systems) can be ignored, thus significantly reducing the clinician's capacity to generate a comprehensive profile of the individual and their difficulties, therefore limiting important opportunities for intervention.

The aim of this book is to bring awareness to the theoretical and practical opportunities and values for mental health professionals, in considering atypical information when adapting typical formulation models. Such awareness may help to expand the basis for how mental health practitioners go about understanding the distress that their clients experience. In doing so, the hypothesis is set that additional 'points of access' to the clients distress, symptoms or narrative may enhance not just the formulation of symptoms, but also the nature of consequent intervention strategies adopted. Underpinning this objective, is the premise that practices in mental health services have been dominated by a constraint in thinking and professional behaviour associated with an over-reliance on formulaic diagnostic categories, which ignore significantly important information generated in routine professional encounters.

Typical approaches have often constrained a freedom of conceptualisation in how mental health practitioners engage with patients, service users and clients. Arguably, professionals have become too tentative in choosing not to complement traditional approaches that would build formulations that are as comprehensive as possible. It is likely that this has been driven by external resource influences which, by definition, cannot understand the form and function of mental well-being and mental distress. Thus, it is preferable to screen, administer tests, look for information on symptoms, and reduce data load to that which fits with preordained but contested disorders, and to diagnose rather than take into account the vast volume of information that emerges in therapeutic sessions that have little to do with symptoms and disorders. And so, for example, the client who reports being depressed will be interviewed about depression and not about how he learned to play as a child, which would give insight into a host of rich data streams related to freedom of expression, creativity, problem solving, emotional regulation, sibling relationships, social network building and overall development of self.

The capacity to generate, capture and utilise information about well-founded psychological constructs and principles in routine therapeutic dialogue would be a useful start in assisting the client. To shift attention from symptoms of distress and disorder by facilitating open exploration of parts of the story of life not normally seen as relevant to well-being. This approach would focus alternatively from symptom oriented self-identifying strategies that bind clients into social expectations about what is right and wrong with who they are. Most importantly, it would assist clients and professionals to apportion balance and care when determining what factors are relevant, salient, accurate and important when working on a formulation of the information that is generated during therapeutic engagement.

In constructing a more broad-based formulation, it will become obvious to both parties what components of the client's story are missing, what parts are only partially accessible from conscious memory, what parts have been retrospectively added to 'complete the circle' and what parts appear implausible, inaccurate or based in thinking errors. A professional encounter orientated in this manner, will generate a type of dialogue that in addition to traditional approaches to information processing and management, will raise interesting and testable hypotheses that can assist in understanding 'stuck' points in therapy, difficulties within the therapeutic relationship, low motivation or inability to engage in particular approaches.

For example, the adult who learned as a child that play was equated with invasive sexual abuse will not readily access information pertaining to creating fun or interest-sharing opportunities that are necessary to buffer against mental distress. A formulation that focuses attention on increasing social networks will therefore only serve to raise stress, which obviously will be avoided by the client even if it makes logical sense to him. However, a formulation that focuses on reducing the trauma experienced in social networks or that focuses on empowering the client in decision making to stay safe will at least go beyond the prescription of, 'join a club' or 'increase hobbies and interests' that can be implicit in the words and actions of well-intentioned practitioners.

Formulation is the key tool for both initiating and sustaining change in psychological therapeutic work. The British Psychological Society is succinct in its 2017 iteration of what formulation is – 'the summation and integration of the knowledge that is acquired by the assessment process' (British Psychological Society, 2017). Thus, one accepted purpose of a formulation is to encapsulate a client's main problems, illustrate the relationship between client's difficulties, explain how difficulties developed from a psychological perspective and guide psychological intervention (Johnstone and Dallos, 2013).

And therein presents a problem – the conceptual basis for formulation has been constrained so that *'difficulties'* are understood better. Not so that *'people'* are understood better. Hence it makes sense that difficulties, distress, and disorder become the focus of assessment, formulation and intervention. The intellectual and practical cost is that other information, data and material are deemed to be irrelevant, unimportant, and unusable in clinical and other professional settings. This book sets out to challenge this consequence by arguing for a space for information outside of rigid theoretical models of disease and disorder to be considered.

Whilst formulation has consistently been described as being inherently dynamic, ever-changing and 'moment in time' based, it has become coupled with the evolving tendency to present human distress in categorizable format, primarily through the influence of, or over-reliance, on diagnostic conceptualisations and intervention manuals. Such methodologies are not necessarily bad in and of themselves, but what is of concern, is that the significant majority of client data that practitioners are exposed to is left unused in the formulation of the distress with which they present. It becomes the detritus of the clinical interviewing process, seen as vaguely relevant but not usually scientific; seen as interesting but not professionally valuable; seen as partial voyeurism, a soft data story but clinically irrelevant.

Interview schedules, screening instruments, psychometric tests and open-ended clinical interviews generate and collect vast amounts of data that cannot be added to the structures and confines of pre-determined categories, diagnoses or labelled clinical frameworks. Therefore, this information is either ignored or treated as anecdotal and less relevant to the distress of the client. Over time, it is then forgotten or is diluted in memory as symptoms that fit with models of practice, or predominant theories play centre stage in how a service, a team or an individual practitioner perceives the needs of the client.

Practitioners in mental health, regardless of discipline, theoretical orientation or ethos at best do not routinely find time or justification to consider the full range of information that is made available to them, or at worst don't know how to. Or perhaps they don't know that it can be validly used to complement current formulation models. For example, clinical psychology – as practised in mental health services – in its endeavour to apply its science to the assessment, diagnosis and treatment of psychological distress, regularly falls short in examining issues beyond the presenting problems of the client. There are few clinical tools used to assess the spiritual world of the person but many tools to assess his depression. As a science based profession, it often struggles to address the usable context of the abstract internal and external environment of the person. In particular, it fails to comprehensively account for and use obvious experiences that fall outside of the neat categories of behaviour, thought, emotion and biology, exclusively coupled to the symptoms of the presenting problem.

As a comparator, client-centered psychotherapeutic approaches will manage the experience of client as the primary valid perspective for understanding distress, and be less concerned about the objective opinion of an 'outside' professional, despite their training and experience, and despite research that clearly shows how poor we are at generating an external view of our own internal world. Neither discipline is wrong in their respective approaches – it is just that there is more on offer, readily available and often easier to use, as it lacks the burdensome weight of the presenting distress.

Formulating psychological distress as partly being linked to poor nutrition or lack of physical activity, immediately opens avenues of potential activation of behavioural change outside of the symptoms being reported, if that is how the client learns best. That same client may not benefit at all from sessions of talk-only therapy that is focused on learning from emotional experience. So the formulation needs to be built around how the client makes sense of experiences, how the client eats, how the client shops, how the client exercises, who taught the client about these experiences, or indeed, who didn't. When constructed in this manner, that formulation is different from one that solely sees distress in terms of reduced appetite, low mood, or problematic sexual functioning, with a focus on changing these.

The lack of capacity to use all information generated in professional encounters is important not only for the purpose of comprehensive and complete understanding of mental distress, but also in terms of ethical competence and practice. The simple but profoundly important ethical principle of being responsible means that the welfare of the client is paramount in all engagement with professionals. That welfare can only be held in the highest regard if all pertinent information is used to further an understanding of distress. Or, that it is ensured that only pertinent information is gathered so that the value and privacy of the client's story is protected from tangential interest. If professionals do not or cannot use information with regard to fundamental human experiences such as sexuality or spirituality, how responsible are their motivations in claiming to have created a thorough understanding of a client's depression or anxiety? Indeed do professionals become subject to that ever-present attention bias central to most psychological distress – that of selective attention? Or of only using information that fits will pre-conceived ideas of what may or may not precipitate and perpetuate a client's psychological distress?

The problematic methodology of how formulation is currently used by professionals is made obvious when it is taken into account that healthy people do not categorise their wellness solely in terms of the absence of symptoms in their behaviour, emotion and thinking. A range of human experiences such as expectations of what self is and how spirituality influences responses, make the story of what a person experiences in their daily life. Often, in the clinical domain, the world of the existential experience is seen as the remit of others, like professionals in psychology, counselling and psychotherapy fields not directly involved in the harsh reality of day-to-day mental health services. It does not belong in the clinical world of state funded health services; and in the insurance driven world of private enterprise, is seen as relevant only if directly attached to clinically proven disorders. Even with the current fascination with and influence of positive psychology, the basis of practice for most clinicians' remains rooted in more traditional categorical approaches to mental health that reflect disorder-formulation, rather than person-formulation models of understanding mental health.

Each of the chapters in this book aims to probe the curiosity of the practitioner, into examining how data routinely available in the course of their daily work can be understood in the context of mental distress, and then used as one of the array of variables that constitute a working formulation. It is hoped that the information in each chapter will assist in setting up an architecture of connections so that clients become learners of their personal story, by attending to more than the information related to symptoms, diagnoses, and prognosis.

The aim of the book is not to dismiss current evidence-based approaches to formulating mental distress, but to add to them and stretch their capacity for a fuller account that will highlight potential for effective and targeted intervention, often outside of the norms of manualised exercises or indeed the norms of the therapy room. Current and traditional approaches to formulation help to organise what is often chaotic, disordered and random personal information and experiences, into frameworks that at least offer the potential for educating and treating psychological conditions. Stretching these frameworks will test their efficacy as therapeutic tools and more importantly, give a platform for readily available clinical information to be used in a novel way to target symptoms of psychological distress.

For the most part in this book, formulation is seen as an interactive, vibrant activity whereby the practitioner begins to understand the client and engage them in the therapeutic process (Johnstone and Dallos, 2013). It is based on an assumption that most professionals will work to generate a co-construction of a formulation within the professional encounter, primarily utilising the therapeutic dialogue generated between the client and mental health practitioner. While this dialogue can validly be generated from structured interviews, technique-based practices or codified diagnostic structure, it often is the mechanism by which people communicate and understand their personal world (Linell, 2009) that offers rich, personally meaningful data which addresses core experiences about themselves and their world. It is assumed that by developing a strong therapeutic relationship using core clinical skills, the practitioner can begin to foster a therapeutic dialogue with the client. Through this therapeutic dialogue, the client's main difficulties and factors influencing the client's distress including personality factors can be identified. This information can then be synthesised with relevant psychological models to develop an integrative comprehensive formulation that is meaningful to the client (Johnstone and Dallos,

2013; BPS, 2017). The constructing and sharing of a formulation with a client serves to strengthen the therapeutic relationship and can be a powerful positive therapeutic intervention (Johnstone and Dallos, 2013) in and of itself.

This book proposes that by extending the base for formulation, an environment and atmosphere of reciprocal learning can be created – the practitioner learning more about the client using information from both formal and informal channels of communication; and the client learning more about themselves than simply a categorisation of symptoms.

Although perhaps not considered a learning theory, the concept of informal learning could be deemed a significant idea within adult learning literature. 'Informal learning is an ubiquitous process that people undertake throughout their lives' (Biesta et al., 2011, p. 29). It could be viewed as a part of everyday life. Hodgekinson et al. (2008) refer to the process of changing, strengthening, or transforming one's disposition through lifelong and often informal learning as a process of becoming. Changes commonly experienced in the lives of adults, such as in relation to work roles, leisure activities, relationships with others, and belief systems are referred to by Biesta et al. (2011) as forming 'parts of a web of activity and meaning in which learning is deeply implicated' (p. 29). Hence, informal learning could be seen as a means by which a client has developed into the individual they present as in therapy. However, the embedded nature of informal learning in adult life make it virtually unfeasible to assess and record (Straka, 2004; Biesta et al., 2011).

In today's society of constant change and global development, everyday life has become a place of constant social change (Nicolaides, 2015), which has been termed 'Liquid Modernity' (Bauman, 2006). It appears that it is the constancy, pace and multi-directional focus of change that marks this particular phase of human evolution apart from earlier generational experiences. Societal architecture, that has been relatively stable for generations appears permeable, fluid and less open to prediction. Liquid modernity has been suggested to create ambiguity for many adults presenting in an adult mental health setting (Nicolaides, 2015). This may take the form of 'an encounter with an appearance of reality that is at first unrecognizable, oblique, simultaneously evoking fear of "no-cognition" and the potential hope for multiple meanings irresolvable by reference to context alone' (Nicolaides, 2015, p. 179). This suggests a close connection between learning and client distress, particularly during this time of Liquid Modernity. The ambiguity experienced, however positively thought out, to give rise to new learning and the development of a new way of living within a changing society and intelligent action, may develop from a connection to ambiguity (Yorks and Nicolaides, 2013; Nicolaides, 2015).

Significant informal learning has been shown in adults from their own life story, a term named 'narrative learning'. The capacity to learn from one's own life and narrative has been suggested as not universal, but a learned skill (Biesta et al., 2011). The opportunity for adults to narrate their own life story may be an 'important vehicle for narrative learning' (Biesta et al., 2011, p. 13) and as crucial in the articulation of a sense of self. This finding could suggest the importance and potential learning from providing a space for clients to narrate their stories, and to perhaps allow adequate space for this during clinical interviews and throughout therapy, to facilitate the clients' learning from their own lives. This framework of informal learning may be usefully applied to clients presenting with the experience of ambiguity, and could be used to facilitate a formulation of their difficulties, as well as giving a hopeful prediction of future learning through this connection to ambiguity. The idea that adult clients are being presented with this concept of liquid modernity could also be employed as a way of formulating client distress.

In this book, each chapter reflects some variation in how formulation is defined, conceptualised and practiced. This is intentional, as practitioners from different theoretical orientations (even within the same discipline) will operationalise their therapeutic engagements in different ways. Similarly, with an overall aim of broadening the concept of formulating, the place for the client's role in generating meaning of their distress is respected by acknowledging the many variations that they bring to even the most rigid of mechanisms for assessment and diagnosis. Hence, no one definition of formulation is ultimately presented as the capstone target for practice, albeit that common premises can be seen across many of the chapters, given that authors and the editor practice in the field of clinical psychology.

Neuroscience

This chapter is included to set a backdrop to how all practitioners need to consider how one of the fastest growing research paradigms in the field of mental health in recent years impacts professional practice. Research has examined the role that genes, proteins, neurotransmitters, structural, functional, and interconnectivity abnormalities within the brain play in mental health and illness. It examines the utility of incorporating a neuroscience perspective into case formulation within mental health practice and shows that the maximal utility of such findings is through its synthesis with other aspects of the assessment process. The chapter is a reminder that what we deal with and try to understand as practitioners is often heavily influenced by a "back story" that is becoming more accessible with technological and neuroscientific advances.

Meaning making

Understanding and deconstructing how people make sense of their world and the lives they live is both fascinating and clinically rewarding, as it reveals the multiplicity of factors that influence how distress is perceived and subsequently managed. Approaches to how meaning-making is understood as well as how it can be integrated into assessment and formulation is considered in this chapter. The chapter prompts the practitioner to consider that in the therapeutic relationship, both parties bring their templates for making sense of the world and deconstructing this with a client can create opportunities for learning about how psychological distress is experienced and maintained.

Personality

This chapter examines theoretical understandings of personality and how it is a fundamental contributor to valid formulations that capture the essence of what it means to be a person. The impact of personality on mental health is considered, as well as how it can be integrated into a formulation to ensure that a comprehensive perspective of the client and their difficulties is captured. Specific psychological disorders will be presented in the context of personality factors. The chapter also brings to awareness, that as personality factors do not relate solely to the client, dynamic factors between the practitioner and the client need to be addressed to understand what happens in the professional relationship.

Sexuality

This chapter discusses historical and current theory on sexuality from a psychological perspective and describes some of the potential for considering the sexual world of the client in formulation and highlight examples for therapeutic dialogue that may capture the nature of relevant information. The aim of the chapter is to guide the practitioner towards creating an open therapeutic dialogue on what is often kept on the periphery of clinical interviewing, even though it is a core element of human experience.

Spirituality

This chapter introduces the experience of spirituality and highlights both theoretical and practical applications in formulations of mental health difficulties. It sets out pertinent issues with existential experiences and aims to inform and educate the practitioner in at least considering how these factors influence the psychological makeup of the individual, and how working with such experiences may help facilitate change in a non-traditional manner. It is a deliberate inclusion in this book, in an effort to address an imbalance in understanding psychological functioning, which in recent history has been oriented to hard-fact, tangible experience only.

Diet and nutrition

The aim of this chapter is to highlight how diet and nutrition factors can add to the psychological formulation process by complementing traditional models of constructing formulation. The chapter highlights specifically how these factors can directly impact both well-being and distress. It explores how diet and nutrition can be merged into formulation and proposes specific questions that may be useful in clinical interviews to enhance formulation.

Physical activity

The aim of this chapter is to highlight how non-clinical variables related to physical activity, sport and exercise, can add to the psychological formulation process by complementing traditional models of constructing formulation. Sport and exercise is used as a working example of an area of a person's life likely to be considered low in clinical relevance, but high in potential for impacting positively on formulation. Of course, any area of interest could reasonably have been included here in terms of accessing information that may related to hobbies, social connection, meaning and purpose. Sport and exercise was chosen given its dominance as a hobby in society in general, but also because activity is one of the factors that becomes impacted upon negatively when psychological imbalance becomes psychological distress or disorder.

Sleep

The aim of this chapter is to examine one central aspect of daily functioning that is not typically incorporated into psychological formulation – that of sleep. The rationale behind incorporating sleep as a key variable in formulation will be explored through its function, its impact on various psychological processes and how it relates to mental health. The influence of sleep on emotion will be examined and its importance in formulating and understanding of distress will be highlighted.

Through these chapters, this book aims to address the imbalance created by only using disorder based or symptom oriented data to construct formulations that can guide intervention, by adapting a psychological approach to the understanding of basic but core experiences, that rarely find their way into standard or standardised assessment and treatment approaches. It sets out current thinking and evidence for a range of atypical concepts related to both well-being and distress. It highlights approaches and tools for designing best practice formulations based on what we have learnt from evidence based research.

Above all, it aims to bring added awareness to the richness of usable, meaningful information generated in routine professional encounters between practitioner and client.

REFERENCES

Bauman, Z. 2006. *Liquid Times: Living in an Age of Uncertainty.* Malden, MA: Polity.

Biesta, G. J. J., Field, J., Hodkinson, P., Macleod, F. J., & Goodson, I. F. 2011 *Improving Learning through the Lifecourse: Learning Lives.* Oxon, U.K: Routledge.

British Psychological Society. BPS Practice Guidelines 2017. Accessible at www.bps.org.uk

Brown, S. & Völlm, B. 2013. Case formulation in personality disordered offenders: Views from the front line. *Criminal Behaviour and Mental Health*, 23(4), 263–273.

Dallos, R. & Stedmon, J. 2014. Systemic formulation: Mapping the family dance, in Johnstone, L. and Dallos, R., eds., *Formulation in Psychology and Psychotherapy: Making Sense of People's Problems.* London: Routledge, 67–95.

Dudley, R. & Kuyken, W. 2014. Case formulation in cognitive behavioural therapy: A principle-driven approach, in Johnstone, L. and Dallos, R., eds., *Formulation in Psychology and Psychotherapy: Making sense of people's problems*, 2nd ed. Hove: Routledge, pp. 18–44.

Hodgekinson, P., Ford, G., Hodgekinson, H., & Hawthorne, R. 2008. Retirement as a learning process. *Educational Gerontology*, 34, 167–184.

Johnstone, L. & Dallos, R. 2013. *Formulation in Psychology and Psychotherapy: Making Sense of People's Problems*. London: Routledge.

Kuyken, W., Padesky C.A., & Dudley, R. 2009. *Collaborative Case Conceptualization: Working Effectively with Clients in Cognitive-Behavioral Therapy*. New York: Guilford Publications.

Leiper, R. 2014. Psychodynamic formulation: Looking beneath the surface, in Johnstone, L. and Dallos, R., eds., *Formulation in Psychology and Psychotherapy: Making Sense of People's Problems*. London: Routledge, 45–66.

Linell, P. 2009. *Rethinking Language, Mind, and World Dialogically*. Charlotte NC: Information Age Publishing.

Nicolaides, A. 2015. Generative learning: Adults learning within ambiguity. *Adult Education Quarterly*, 65(3), 179–195.

Straka, G. A. 2004. *Informal Learning: Genealogy, Concept, Antagonism and Questions*. Bremen: Institut Technik und Bildung.

Yorks, L. & Nicolaides, A. 2013. Toward an Integral Approach for Evolving Mindsets for Generative Learning and Timely Action in the Midst of Ambiguity. *Teachers College Record*. 115.

Chapter 2

Meaning making in formulation

Eva Usher and Patrick Ryan

CHAPTER TOPICS

- Review of the theoretical models that meaning making can be conceptualised through
- Exploration of quantitative and qualitative approaches to assessing meaning making
- Review of therapeutic dialogue issues such as semantics, cognitive heuristics and symptom identification when assessing meaning making with clients
- The role of meaning making in the collaborative partnership of recovery

Introduction

How clients derive and make sense of their particular life story is central to how a useful formulation of their presenting problem can be constructed. Historical approaches in mental health were heavily influenced by the identity of the practitioner as the expert, with a reduced focus on attempting to understand how a client generates meaning about their health or illness profile. For a client to understand what underlies their distress, they also need to have insight into how they understand and make sense of the interactions between psychological variables that permeate their lives. A useful literature on meaning making exists that stands outside of research specifically related to mental health functioning, and this chapter explores some such theoretical orientations, the range of qualitative and quantitative measures for meaning making and the complexities of considering such a non-clinical topic in formulation.

The current shift towards transdiagnostic approaches has unearthed processes that are significant influences on mental health functioning. Meaning making, the processes by which people understand themselves, their environment, their relationship to the environment, and when violations of this understanding occurs, ways to respond to it, is one such process. According to Camus (1955) we are influenced by a "nostalgia for unity," a search for an absolute certainty, effortlessly connecting things up. Several studies have shown how this search for meaning has a positive impact on well-being and mental health (Samman, 2007; Steger, Kashdan, & Oishi, 2008; Day, Hanson, Maltby, Proctor, & Wood, 2010; Kobau, Sniezek, Zack, Lucas, & Burns, 2010; Seligman, 2011).

Across this same literature there is a lack of consensus on the operationalisation of "meaning" and "meaning making" (Frankl, 1985; Park, 2013). Before considering the possibility of the use of meaning within a formulation, the practitioner is bombarded with a litany of definitions, binary and dimensional, to choose from. Definitions range from epistemic meaning (the what is) to teleological meaning (the why and what next) (Wong, 2012); provisional meaning (obtained through daily tasks), and ultimate meaning (a deeper belief system) (Frankl, 2006/1985); cosmic meaning (sense of coherence; whether life has a design/pattern superior to oneself), and terrestrial meaning (sense of purpose) (Yalom, 1980); existential and implicit meaning (Wong, 1998); comprehension (sense making and understanding of one's life) to purpose (long term aspirations) (Steger, 2012); situational and global meaning (Park & Folkman, 1997; Park, 2010, 2013).

Once the definitional labyrinth has been deconstructed, there is a myriad of theoretical perspectives to consider, each having its own hypotheses of the core processes involved in meaning. Some of these theoretical perspectives will be outlined with a view to raising awareness of how the practitioner and the client may engage in understanding psychological distress, individually and jointly.

Constructivist psychology

In constructivist psychology, individuals are active agents and the self is an active, organising process rather than an entity, which generates meaning in life for survival purposes. Meaning making is a core activity and involves ordering processes in an emotional, tacit and categorical manner. It is influenced by social symbolic processes—"web of relationships"—which are determined by language, symbols and expressed through stories. Constructivist approaches differ on emphasis of role for the individual or community, linguistic, cultural or private influences on meaning making. Knowledge and meaning are "contextually verifiable rather than universally valid, and linguistically generated and socially negotiated rather than cognitively and individually produced" (Chiari & Nuzzo, 1996).

George Kelly (1970) was one of the first to formally integrate the constructivist approach and psychotherapy. Kelly (1970) posited that individuals use "personal constructs" to predict how others behave through a hierarchy of constructs, from superordinate to subordinate, and core to peripheral constructs. Individuals engage in cyclical process known as the "experience cycle" (Kelly, 1970), where they hypothesise and test out their constructs of the world. In formulation, the practitioner is tasked with uncovering the unique and particular inferred constructs, whether they are loose or tightly construed and "subsuming" these constructs without interference by their own constructs (Kelly, 1970). Personal construct theory has been further developed to incorporate interpersonal construing (Leitner, Faidley, & Celentana, 2000), where ideas and hypotheses pertaining to the relationships with others can be explored—especially useful in psychological therapies where the professional relationship is core to whether many interventions are effective or not.

However, constructivist psychology lacks a single consistent coherent theoretical orientation, or approved psychotherapy, or set of techniques. Constructivist psychotherapy can be seen as a psychological mindset rather than a set of formalised procedures and techniques, but nonetheless useful in explaining health and distress for those who perceived their world through this type of lens.

Existential perspective

The existential perspective on meaning proposes that each human being has an intrinsic motivation towards a quest for meaning, "for life expansion but also a powerful capacity for personal transformation" (Frankl, 1985). Individuals are conceived of as "meaning seeking and meaning making creatures" (Frankl, 1985) particularly in the face of suffering. Meaning in suffering is conceived of as an opportunity, to possess "tragic optimism" (Frankl, 1985)—a philosophy that echo's Nietzsche (1955) dictum "He who has a why to live for can bear almost any how." Individuals can be confronted with conflicts of the "givens of existence" such as meaninglessness, death, isolation and loneliness (Yalom, 1980) and actively construct a purpose from this rather than passively accepting the status quo.

Logotherapy, "therapy through meaning," was one of the earlier forms of existential psychotherapy. It proposes three basic tenets, that individuals have the capacity for "freedom of will" (to choose how to respond to a situation, however difficult), for will to be meaning (be drawn forward to fulfill future meaning) and for meaning of life (to find meaning in the most awful circumstance; a spiritual meaning) (Frankl, 1985). If a quest for meaning is blocked then an individual can experience existential frustration, a sense of meaningless, boredom, emptiness and be in an "existential vacuum" (Frankl, 1985).

In existential perspectives, the practitioner can adopt an existential phenomenological approach to formulation, considering how the client's experience fits in with wider existence, and to co-experience and see the clients reality from a wide range of perspectives, rather than just the presence or absence of symptoms. Criticisms have been levelled against existential approaches including that logotherapy is authoritarian and anti-reductionist in its approach, and against clinical practitioners for its inability to be empirically tested and be researched. It also demonstrates a narrative that appears culturally biased in how goal fulfillment is described (Wong, 1998) and its central concept of meaning, that is discoverable rather than made (Frankl, 2000) is at odds with research which indicates that meaning is constructed, not clarified (Park, 2010). It is this conflict, that can be useful to practitioners in formulation—constructing a formulation based on existential principles will work for clients who see their lives as a quest for meaning, whilst it offers little to the client who actively assumes that they are constructing their own pathway to health.

Self-determination perspective

Self Determination Theory is a theory of human motivation and personality development (Ryan & Deci, 2000). It integrates humanistic-existential theory and social-personality processes, and considers meaning making as choosing a life goal and adjusting accordingly to enhance the probability of achieving it. Self determination theory identifies the psychological need for autonomy, competence and relatedness (the three basic psychological needs) as important to experiencing meaning (Ryan & Deci, 2000). The processes involved in meaning making include higher order cognitive activities such as assimilation, integration and symbolization. The theory identifies the role of social contextual factors in aiding and undermining the integration of new meaning. Routledge and Arndt (2009) reported that when participants were primed for creativity before mortality, they expressed more interest in novel, social, cultural and environmental experiences.

Wong (1998, 2012) proposed a dual systems model of personal meaning based on logotherapy and self-determination theory "with the aim to optimise positive transformations of the individual." It is a meaning centred, self-regulatory system for meaning seeking, meaning making and meaning reconstruction which incorporates effective coping and stress management. According to Wong (2012), positive and negative experiences, and approach and avoidance systems co-exist reflecting different emotional-behavioural and neurophysiology processes. Different systems predominate in different contexts. However, optimal outcome depends on effective interaction between all systems, where too much emphasis on any one system is maladaptive. The model mediates between interactions of "PURE" (Purpose, Understanding, Responsible action and Enjoyment, which define meaning); "ABCDE" (the Acceptance, Belief, Commitment, Discovering and Evaluation, transformative intervention strategy); and "tragic optimism" (restoration of hope in hopeless situation through acceptance, "belief, courage, religious faith and self transcendence"), creating a meaning centred "positive triad," to ensure resilience and flourishing (Wong, 1998, 2012). This transtheoretical model has become established as Meaning Centred Counselling Therapy.

Meaning Centred Counselling Therapy (Wong, 2012) focuses on developing existential insight and psychotherapy skills. It is an integrated, holistic, relational, multicultural framework arising out of two complementary models—Meaning management theory and the Dual system model. Meaning management theory explores the underlying processes involved in the regulation of one's life and meaning; how an individual construes the world and the related cognitive processes such as stress appraisal and decision making; goal setting and making choices (Wong, 2012). In parallel to Wong's research, the link between cognitive process and meaning making was being explored from a personality and cognitive psychology perspective.

Personality and cognitive psychology perspective

Within the personality and cognitive psychology literature, an individual's narrative content, structure and theme are critical to meaning making. McAdams

(2012) conceives personality to be constituted of three levels (dispositional, characteristic adaptations and integrative life stories), which all contribute to meaning making.

At the dispositional level, traits such as extroversion, hardiness and positive emotionality are more likely to enhance sense of meaning in life, particularly, in adversity (Maddi, 1998; Schnell & Becker, 2006). According to Maddi (1998) the meaning-based construct of hardiness, which is composed of three acquired traits: commitment (sustained engagement in social sphere), control (sense of ability to accomplish) and challenge (change as interesting), acts as a buffer against the experience of anxiety.

The characteristic level is focused on the context where individuals create their meaning, through social roles, personal goals, projects and strategies (Arnett, 2000; Freund & Riediger, 2006). At the integrative level, McAdams (2012) emphasised narrative as essential in the creation of a meaningful life. Particular themes of contamination and redemption within life stories/ narratives were deemed the most significant in understanding a person's meaning making. Life stories with more redemption (considering negative events as turning out positively) report higher life satisfaction and emotional well-being (Lodi-Smith et al., 2009). The more plentiful contamination themes (where good things go bad and stay bad), the higher the levels of psychological distress (Lodi-Smith, Geise, Roberts, & Robins, 2009). Narrative coherence (temporal and causal structure) and use of cognitive processing words such as "cause, know, ought, realize and understand" are indicators of meaning making and have been found to be positively related to mental health and well-being (Frattaroli, 2006; Fivush, Sales, & Bohanek, 2008; Reese, Haden, Baker-Ward, Bauer, Fivush, & Ornstein, 2011). In this respect the practitioner would have to regard formulation as a dialogue incorporating both the problem and its exceptions (Carr, 2012; Harper & Moss, 2003).

KEY POINT

The utility of meaning making can be influenced by the nature of life stories: Redemption stories have been shown to lead to positive psychological outcomes whereby contamination themes may act to prolong distress.

However, studies have found that individuals who engage in high levels of cognitive processing in the retelling of stressful events actually show lower levels of well-being, and it can be an indicator of continued distress (Fivush, Marin, Crawford, Brewin, & Reynolds, 2007; Marin, Bohanek, & Fivush, 2008). What seems to be significant, is the *kind* of meaning that is made. Literature on post traumatic growth offers more insight into meaning making processes.

Post traumatic growth

The most relevant conceptualizations of post traumatic growth and meaning are the models of post traumatic growth as an outcome of a traumatic event (explicit model) (Tedeschi & Calhoun, 1996, 2004) or as a coping strategy (implicit model) (Park & Folkman, 1997; Park, 2010). In the Tedeschi and Calhoun (1996, 2004) functional descriptive model, post traumatic growth involves a process of positive psychological change as consequence of negative events. According to the model, a traumatic event occurs which impacts higher order goals and beliefs, leading to an initial response of automatic rumination which can be influenced by pre-trauma variables (distal factors). Successful coping brings about constructive, deliberate rumination and thinking (proximal factors) which in turn initiates personal growth. The model has five aspects of positive change: (1) increased sense of personal strength, (2) deepening of personal relationships, (3) increased appreciation for life, (4) enhanced spirituality and (5) openness to new possibilities (Tedeschi & Calhoun, 1996, 2004).

On the other hand, both Park (2010) and Pals and McAdams (2004) argue that post traumatic growth is a form of meaning making involving personal reflection and meaningful causal connections, in the context of stress and coping. According to Park and Folkman (1997; Park, 2010) model, a stressful event involves conflict between global and situational meaning. Global meaning involves a sustained understanding of past, present and future based on an assumption of order (beliefs about self, world, and self in the world) and motivation (Park & Folkman, 1997). Situational meaning is that which occurs as a result of interaction between global meaning (worldview) and an event/encounter. The conflict in meanings initiates the individual to identify coping strategies which are informed by their global meaning, in the search for meaning. During this process the individual will either change their global meaning, or reappraise the situation to reduce its incongruence with global meaning (assimilation). If neither of these two processes occurs, then the result is rumination. The application of this model is particularly prevalent within literature on coping responses to HIV/AIDS (Jacobson, Luckhaupt, Delaney, & Tsevat, 2006; Plattner & Meiring, 2006). Meaning making in post traumatic growth reflects a coping strategy independent of event type, and that increased distress requires increased "efforts after meaning" (Park, 2010).

However, findings are mixed in relation to post traumatic growth and correlations with depression and anxiety (Grubaugh & Resick, 2007; Boals, Steward, & Schuettler, 2010). An increasing number of studies have found that higher post traumatic growth, meaning making, thematic and chronological coherence is concurrently related to higher levels of intrusion, hyperarousal and global PTSD symptom and stress (Helgeson, Reynolds, & Tomich, 2006; Boals et al., 2010). Zoellner and Maercker (2006) noted that post traumatic growth is not necessarily a sign of having found meaning nor having benefitted from finding meaning.

KEY POINT

Meaning making can act as a coping strategy after post traumatic growth. However, there is insufficient evidence linking greater meaning making capabilities with improved long-term mental health outcomes in clients.

Having given consideration to the various theoretical perspectives that meaning making can be conceptualised through, the focus now turns to quantitative and then qualitative methods of meaning making that the practitioner can utilise in the process of clinical formulation.

Psychometric measures and meaning making

Quantitative instruments for meaning making have been hampered by the difficulty with operationalising the construct of meaning making. As previously mentioned, the literature proposes numerous definitions of meaning making and sources of meaning. There is limited comparison of constructs, and lack of clarity about whether meaning is a single construct or multifaceted with multiple constructs (Waters, Shallcross, & Fivush, 2013). While there has been a surge in quantitative measures in recent years, few have addressed discrepancy/violation of global belief, or discrepancy between global and situational meaning (Waters et al., 2013). Nevertheless, measures of meaning can be useful in identifying a deficit/ imbalance in meaning and, where it is sourced, can provide information on areas for intervention and changes over time (Steger, 2012). Below is a brief overview of some possible measures for clinical application and as an adjunct to clinical formulation.

Meaning in life questionnaire

This questionnaire is based on the premise that meaning is "the sense made of, and significance felt regarding, the nature of one's being and existence" (Steger, Frazier, Oishi, & Kaler, 2006). It is a 10-item scale that is composed of two subscales: presence (subjective sense that one's life is meaningful), and search (drive to find meaning in life). Internal consistency of the subscales is between 0.86 and 0.88.

Post traumatic growth inventory (Tedeschi & Calhoun, 1996)

Post traumatic Growth Inventory is a 21-item questionnaire used to measure positive outcome following a traumatic event (Tedeschi & Calhoun, 1996). It consists of five subscales and scores can range from, 21–126. It has internal consistency of 0.90, moderate test-retest reliability $r = 0.71$ and validity (Tedeschi & Calhoun, 1996).

Personal meaning profile (Wong, 1998)

This instrument consists of 57 items which aim to measure respondent's perception of personal meaning in their lives. Its design was based on implicit theories via a deductive approach whereby categories emerged out of participant's responses rather than a priori categories or theoretical biases. The instrument was established over a period of four consecutive studies which included factor analysis and component analysis. The greater the score the "more successful a person is in approximating the ideally meaningful life" (Wong, 2012). The more sources a person derives meaning from highlights the "breadth of meaning seeking" (Wong, 1998). The level of meaning across each subscale portrays the balance in meaning seeking. Elevated subscales can also indicate if meaning is self-seeking or self-transcended. Overall Cronbach's alpha coefficient is 0.93 and test re-test reliability is 0.85. It has been used in a wide variety of settings from organisational to clinical. A study conducted by Mascaro (2006, cited in Wong, 2012) investigating the relationship between a number of scales indicated that the PMP correlates positively with other psychometric properties. Many studies have highlighted its positive correlation with psychological well-being perceived or otherwise and negative correlation with distress (Wong, 2012). A short form has been established (Personal Meaning Profile B) which consists of 21 items with fewer items in each subscale.

Multidimensional life scale (Edwards, 2007)

Based on a factor analysis of a number of existing meaning measures, 10 "super" factors were established. Internal consistency is 0.70. There is no current information on test-retest reliability. Over the course of the three studies to establish the scale, Edwards (2007) concluded that meaning in life was indeed a multidimensional construct.

The source of meaning and meaning in life questionnaire (Schnell, 2009)

This questionnaire draws on a hierarchical model of meaning with five levels of complexity and is based on action theory (Schnell, 2009). It is a 151-item inventory, including 26 sources of meaning categorised into four dimensions. It incorporates two scales that assess meaningfulness and crisis of meaning. Meaningfulness is based on "an appraisal of one's life as coherent, significant, directed and belonging" (Schnell, 2009). Crisis of meaning involves the "judgement of one's life as empty, pointless and lacking meaning" (Schnell, 2009). It measures presence and search for meaning separately. Laddering and content analysis of interviews was carried out by a team of researchers. Internal consistencies range from 0.83 to 0.93 for the dimensions (M = 0.89), and 0.65 to 0.95 for the scales (M = 0.79). Test-retest stability coefficients for scales at two months are 0.81 and 0.90 for the dimensions. Numerous studies highlight the questionnaire's validity (Gapp & Schnell, 2008; Schnell, 2009).

Spiritual meaning scale (Mascaro, Rosen, & Morey, 2004)

For Mascaro and colleagues (2004), meaning comprises three constructs: Personal meaning, implicit meaning and spiritual meaning. Spiritual meaning is defined as "the extent to which an individual believes that life or some force of which life is a function has a purpose, will, or way in which individuals participate" (Mascaro et al., 2004). The scale consists of 14 Likert format items. Mascaro et al. (2004) demonstrated that the Spiritual Meaning Scale, Personal Meaning Profile (Wong, 1998), and the Life Regard Index (Battista & Almond, 1973, cited in Wong, 2012) explained variance in hope and depression beyond the Big Five personality factors and that all three measures were significantly correlated with each other. The composite measure is a more reliable and valid measure of existential meaning than any of the isolated scales.

Schedule for meaning in life evaluation (Fegg, Kramer, L'hoste, & Borasio 2008)

This schedule is a response generated measure whereby respondents list three to seven areas that provide meaning in their lives and then rate the current level of importance and satisfaction of each area (Fegg et al., 2008). The areas are then assigned to a posteriori categories which emerged out of a cluster analysis of a nationwide survey of 1004 German respondents. A mean value for satisfaction can be ascertained by summing up the satisfaction ratings for each area and dividing by the number of areas. The Cronbach's alpha and test-retest reliability of the satisfaction ratings were high ($r = 0.72$ ($P < 0.001$)). The schedule has a reliability coefficient alpha of 0.89 and high internal consistency. However, Wong (2012) outlines the level of cognitive effort involved in completing items as a limitation.

Meaningful life measure (Morgan & Farsides, 2009)

This 23-item measure consists of five subscales to assess components of personal meaning. These subscales emerged out of a factor analysis of three existing measures: Purpose in Life Scale (Crumbaugh & Maholick, 1969, cited in Wong, 2012), Life Regard Index (Battista & Almond, 1973 cited in Wong, 2012) and Ryff's Psychological Well-being Purpose subscale (Ryff, 1989, cited in Wong, 2012). According to Wong (2012) the measure is a good resource for establishing the antecedents and consequences of specific components of personal meaning. Wong (2012) also identifies its over-emphasis on the purpose of the meaning as a limitation.

Qualitative processes to reveal meaning making

Opportunities for exploring meaning making in clinical assessment are plentiful. Narrative therapy, logotherapy, personal construct and existential therapy have established processes or questions for eliciting meaning. Meaning questions are woven throughout the fabric of the clinical assessment or therapeutic intervention supporting the person into a reflective position. To explore meaning, the practitioner has to do what Husserl (1960) suggests, "bracket," "suspend," "withhold" and "parenthesise" assumptions to consider alternative possibilities. Or, what Spinelli (1989) guides—to mindfully include aspects of phenomenological methodology such as the "rules of description" (describe, don't explain, stay with lived experience) and "rule of horizontalization" (avoid hierarchy of significance/ importance)—into interaction. According to Frankl (1985) "our task is to resort to a phenomenological investigation of the immediate data of actual life experience." Within the therapeutic dialogues in assessment and intervention, the practitioner must not prescribe or ascribe meaning, but rather invite the client into meaning and allow the client to take responsibility for the meaning made. According to Schneider and May (1995), the practitioner reflects back to the client what is heard and what is being intended to say, and as a result of the interpersonal interaction, the practitioner must be open to being transformed by the therapeutic encounter.

From initial contact onwards the practitioner should consider the assumptions within the referral, and hypothesise the implicit dominant and subordinate discourses/narratives (Harper & Spellman cited in Johnstone & Dallos, 2014). At assessment stage, the practitioner can ascertain if there is a problem and, if so, who gets to define it and indeed if the client perceives the issue to be a problem. The emphasis in these approaches is on the interactional process and relationship with the problem rather than a focus on the problem itself. As a result, it is preferable for the practitioner to employ a conversational approach rather than a didactic approach, in order to elicit information that gives insight into how the client is currently making sense of their psychological distress.

KEY POINT

The refining of meaning making within the therapeutic relationship must be developed early between practitioner and client and requires the potential for openness to change on the part of the client.

In narrative therapy, the dialogue is a means to generate experience rather than to gather information. The practitioner does not take the stance of pre-understanding but rather accommodates and uses a space for not knowing. The practitioner can avail of styles such as externalising conversations, deconstructing questions, opening space questions, preference questions, story development questions and meaning questions (Freedman & Combs, 1996; Payne, 2000). Open-ended questions are kept in mind to use in a flexible, conversational manner, but in the context of a therapeutic dialogue.

The practitioner notices the language the client uses to describe the problem (metaphorical or otherwise), then uses the person's language to describe the problem, modify it so that the problem is objectified and ask personal questions about it (Freedman & Combs, 1996; Payne, 2000). The practitioner must aim to explore the "legacy" of the problem, to discover "unique outcomes" or exceptions to the problem's life and enquire about an alternative story (Payne, 2000).

The practitioner can ask the client to describe their relationship with the problem and in doing so explore whether the problem has useful, but difficult to express, purposes. Careful questioning as to whether the problem is experienced as intrinsic and enmeshed with self-concept and identity can be employed. Active listening will help to establish if there is scope to minimise the personalisation of the problem and engage in "externalising conversations" (White & Epston, 1990; Harper & Spellman, 2014).

Within these externalising conversations, the practitioner can use the narrative therapy process of deconstructive questioning/"unpacking" which incorporates three categories of questioning: (1) landscape of action questions (plotting sequence of events in time and characters involved; what have you done to create an identity for yourself without letting past trauma create your identity? How did you get ready to take this step?), (2) landscape of consciousness questions (exploring the motivations, hopes, goals, values, beliefs, characteristics and qualities of self and implication of meanings support) and (3) experience of experience questions (what the person thinks others might be thinking) (Bruner, 1986; White & Epston, 1990). Some examples of such deconstructive questioning include:

"What does it tell you about what suits you as a person?"; "What does it mean that you have accomplished so much in spite of the abuse?"; "What does the history of struggle suggest about what x believes to be important in his life, about what he stands for?"; "If I (the practitioner) was a spectator, what would I have seen you do then that might help me understand how you were able to achieve what you have recently achieved?" "What does it mean to you that this would happen?; What qualities are evident to you now that you took steps to put problem out of your life?"; "What do you think that person believed to take the stand they did?"; "Is there something you have learnt from this that you can take to other aspects of your life?" "What did you know of who you were then that you have lost track of since?" (White, 1995). The practitioner can also explore the role of subjugating and dominant discourses ("What feeds/starves the problem?" "Where did you learn this way of thinking about relationships?" "How did fear so easily coach you to believe that?" "How does the fear know when to get you? (White, 1995)".

This type of circular and Socratic questioning allows the practitioner and client to see a life story and its substories from multiple perspectives. Notice how they construct their stories, become aware of how they use confirming and disconfirming information and learn about limitations of their one narrative and the possibility opened up by other possible narratives.

One alternative strategy the practitioner can engage in is "Re-membering conversations" (Morgan, 2000), assisting the client to reconnect with significant relationships through questions such as: "*Who else knows you stand up to fear?*" "*Can you think of anyone who can tell a story about your commitment to fight injustice/loneliness?*"

From an existential therapy perspective, the therapeutic dialogue will be influenced by where the practitioner is positioned on the dimension of existentialism and meaning—the empirical psychological or the abstract philosophical end of the dimension. The existential approach broadens professional inquiry to look at beliefs about putative resolutions, to explore the world, to consider values and meaning, to focus on the transpersonal dimensions of experience (van Deurzen-Smith, 1997). It seeks to incorporate universalising (an experience that is shared across humanity and to be accepted and faced) rather than individualising (individual disorders to overcome) (van Deurzen, 2002). The practitioner will check for pattern recognition, in the way the individual makes sense of the world—relational and hermeneutic.

Examples of existential humanistic strategies that are useful include:

1. Asking the client what their internal subjective experience tells them: How does it feel when you say that (Schneider & May, 1995); *What's there, slowly now can you describe it, see if you can stay with it a little longer*;
2. Embodied meditation (Schneider & May, 1995), whereby the practitioner explores how the client feels in the moment and in relation to the practitioner (Bugental, 1999);
3. Searching for the words that best describe meaning the person would like life to have (*what good reason to live would you give a murderer should he want to take your life?* (Payne, 2000));
4. Exploring whether a client can consider that every situation has some meaning which creates an opportunity for each individual to examine their attitude to distress;
5. Assessing whether the client can engage in "*dereflection,*" a process of adding an external perspective on an internal experience (Frankl, 1985; Cooper, 2003).

"Miracle" questions can tap into metacognitive mechanisms useful for creating a distance between the person and the problem (*If you could do whatever you want on a daily basis right now and money isn't an issue what would you do? If you were granted three wishes, what would your top three be? If you were able to decide on a future right now what would the ideal life situation be in 3–5 years time?*) (Wong, 2012). "Fast forwarding" (Wong, 2012) can sustain problem solving skills (imagining where a particular individual choice will get them in their life and if they are sure this is what they really want).

Personal construct approaches utilise more structural methods to ascertaining meaning making and level of interpersonal construing (Ugazio, Negri & Fellin, 2015, cited in Johnstone & Dallos, 2014). Making use of the repertory grid technique (Fransella, Bell, & Bannister, 2004) and qualitative grids

(Procter, 2005) to elicit aspects of self (current, ideal and future self) can be useful for those that are more pragmatic in approach to life, and the use of these often prompts a "third person" perspective on even the most personal of issues. Laddering (Hinkle, 1965), where the client is asked "which pole on a construct s/he would prefer to be described by and why" and ABC technique (Tschudi & Winter, 2011), which reviews the implications of the pole of each construct can also assist with therapeutic conversation building.

As outlined, a number of techniques are available to the practitioner, and while technical prowess can be beneficial in assuring clients about the professionalism of the service provider, a reflexive and reflective stance is required as there are a number of issues that can occur in therapeutic dialogues that need to be understood to sustain therapeutic collaboration.

Therapeutic dialogue issues

Within therapeutic dialogues the practitioner needs to be aware of what they bring to the professional encounter that impacts what the client has to make sense of. Hermans (2004) proposed that the practitioner's self be considered as dialogical in nature, "a dynamic multiplicity of (voiced) positions in the landscape of the mind, intertwined as this mind is with the minds of other people." Studies have found that the practitioner is engaged with their "professional" and "experiencing self" during therapeutic encounters and is tasked with managing attention to client process, processing the client's story, focusing on their own process, and managing the therapeutic process (Rober, Elliott, Buysse, Loots, & De Corte, 2008). According to Williams, Polster, Grizzard, Rockenbaugh and Judge (2003) the key to the management of these inner conversations is self-talk. However, it is not just the internal dialogues that are important.

Evidence has emerged that certain disorders have certain dominant semantics, such as patterns related to freedom, goodness, power and belonging (Ugazio, Negri, & Fellin, 2015). The practitioner also needs to be aware of the conversational contexts meaning has developed in; that the meaning presented may be a micro representation of the family and wider culture. Exploration of meaning can facilitate a semantic profile of the client (Ugazio et al., 2015). The practitioner also contributes to the prevalence of critical semantics within the dialogue and can also make proportionally more use of semantics to open up an alternative view (Ugazio et al., 2015).

Similar to traditional formulation and assessment, the practitioner involved in exploring meaning making processes with a client can inadvertently apply cognitive heuristics and biases, as formulated by Tversky and Kahneman (1974). The practitioner operating in the role of professional needs to be aware of the influences of availability bias (putting weight on things that come to mind easily—"children give me reason for living"), confirmatory bias (seeking information that fits pre-existing expectations, e.g., older client finding meaning in religion), illusory correlation and representativeness biases (e.g., spiritual meaning implies they are religious, academic meaning implies they are studious, relatedness meaning implies they are can relate). An even more relevant heuristic to exploring meaning making is the "affect heuristic" (Slovic, Finucane, Peters, & MacGregor, 2002) whereby value laden language generates automatic responses and judgement based on affect (e.g., someone stating they obtain meaning from relationships can generate feelings of comfort in the practitioner). This is further supported by the finding by De Martino, Kumaran, Seymour and Dolan (2006) that emotional systems are involved in mediating decision biases. Therefore, the practitioner needs to be aware of how they make decisions and judgements and how they monitor and regulate this in professional encounters given that clients will experience part of this process and then have to make sense of this also.

Having this approach undoubtedly adds to workload for the practitioner, but if this is so, is it more taxing on the practitioner to have a "meaning mindset" (Wong, 2012) in clinical formulation? Then why bother? Considering "non-clinical" aspects such as meaning making can assist the practitioner to avoid the type of cognitive errors and biases as outlined earlier. By adding meaning making to the compendium of approaches for practitioners, "symptoms" are considered as a process of meaning, and understood in a collaborative sense making process (Harper & Moss, 2003), rather than a target that requires manipulation, standing alone from the context from which it has emerged. This can assist with reducing treatment misalignment as interventions are conceptualised on data that has currency for the client.

Considering meaning making processes in formulation will support case conceptualization irrespective of theoretical orientation and is useful for making and testing predictions that can identify further areas of risk and help with unexplained factors (Butler, 1998 cited in Johnstone & Dallos, 2014). So, for example, practitioners can access information about client's beliefs and misbeliefs; stances and contradictions; values and assumptions that will help generate a comprehensive picture of their health and illness profile. As an ethos, it promotes the idea that the client can be an active contributor to the formulation of their difficulties through a dialogue that offers more than symptom description. It allows the practitioner to unravel "those disembodied ways of speaking that hide their (the client's) biases and prejudices; and those familiar practices of self and of relationship that are subjugating a person's life" (White, 1991). According to Butler (1998 cited in Johnstone and Dallos, 2014) formulation is a process of "negotiating for shared ...meaning" and to ensure the formulation is personally meaningful the practitioner must understand the individual's meaning processes. In order to do this, the practitioner must add to the position of knowing and expertise that comes from being a professional, a space where curiosity and uncertainty can also provide useful insight into psychological distress. Equally, the practitioner must also know when not to explore meaning making systems. For some, this is beyond current capacity, holds little relevance to how they experience their distress, or simply is not of interest.

KEY POINT

Practitioners must take into account clients' own processes, capacity and motivation to explore meaning making in their psychological interventions.

With the amount of adaptation and assimilation service users have to undertake when provided with a formulation, it is crucial to explore how they make sense of their experience. Including a client's meaning making process in clinical formulation offers every individual the "right to a life that is not defined by illness or diagnosis" (Davidson & Strauss, 1992), which involves a service users need to become re-enchanted with life again (Watts, 2012) and "reconnecting with self, others and time" (Kartalova-O'Doherty & Tedstone Doherty, 2010). It creates further opportunities for the collaborative partnership ethos of recovery and is inclusive of social recovery.

In spite of the myriad of perspectives on meaning making, this chapter has provided an overview of the methodological, theoretical and practical considerations to be given when using non-clinical aspects in clinical formulations. It has indicated some parameters for a more comprehensive incorporation of client information that is readily and routinely available in therapeutic encounters to enhance the experience of formulation.

Reflective exercise

Consider your development as a mental health practitioner from your time in education to your current status. Identify key learning moments across this development. How did you make sense of these moments when they occurred? What meaning do these hold for you now? What is the best way for you to understand and communicate any differences between your original meaning and how you experience these now?

REFERENCES

Arnett, J. 2000. Emerging adulthood: A theory of development from the late teens through the twenties. *American Psychologist*, 55, 469–480.

Boals, A., Steward, J., & Schuettler, D. 2010. Advancing our understanding of posttraumatic growth by considering event centrality. *Journal of Loss and Trauma*, 15, 518–533.

Bruner, J. 1986. *Actual Minds, Possible Worlds*. Cambridge, MA: Harvard University Press.

Bugental, J. 1999. *Psychotherapy isn't What You Think: Bringing the Psychotherapeutic Engagement in the Living Moment*. Phoenix AZ: Zeig, Tucker.

Camus, Albert. 1955. *The Myth of Sisyphus*. England: Hamish Hamilton.

Carr, A. 2012. *Family Therapy: Concepts, Process and Practice*, 3rd edn. Chichester: Wiley-Blackwell.

Chiari, G., & Nuzzo, M. 1996. Psychological constructivisms: A metatheoretical differentiation. *Journal of Constructivist Psychology*, 9, 163–184.

Cooper, M. 2003. *Existential Therapies*. London: Sage Publications.

Davidson, L., & Strauss, J. 1992. Sense of self in recovery from severe mental illness. *British Journal of Medical Psychology*, 65, 131–145.

Day, L., Hanson, K., Maltby, J., Proctor, C., & Wood, A. 2010. Hope uniquely predicts objective academic achievement above intelligence, personality, and previous academic achievement. *Journal of Research in Personality*, 44, 550–553.

De Martino, B., Kumaran, D., Seymour, B., & Dolan, R. 2006. Frames, biases, and rational decision-making in the human brain. *Science*, 313, 5787, 684–687.

Edwards, M. 2007. *The dimensionality and construct valid measurement of life meaning*. Unpublished doctoral dissertation, Queen's University, Kingston, ON, Canada.

Fegg, M., Kramer, M., L'hoste, S., & Borasio, G. 2008. The schedule for meaning in life evaluation (SMiLE): Validation of a new instrument for meaning-in-life research. *Journal of Pain and Symptom Management*, 35, 4, 356–564.

Fivush, R., Marin, K., Crawford, M., Brewin, C., & Reynolds, M. 2007. Children's narratives and well-being. *Cognition and Emotion*, 21, 1414–1434.

Fivush, R., Sales, J., & Bohanek, J. 2008. Meaning making in mothers' and children's narratives of emotional events. *Memory*, 16, 579–594.

Frankl, V. 1985. *Man's Search for Meaning*. New York: Washington Square Press.

Frankl, V. 2000. *Recollections: An Autobiography*. New York, NY: Basic Books.

Frankl, V. E. 2006. *Man's Search for Meaning*. Boston: Beacon Press.

Fransella, F., Bell, R., & Bannister, D. 2004. *A Manual for Repertory Grid Technique*, 2nd edn. Chichester: Wiley.

Frattaroli, J. 2006. Experimental disclosure and its moderators: A meta-analysis. *Psychological Bulletin*, 132, 823–865.

Freedman, J., & Combs, G. 1996. *Narrative Therapy: The Social Construction of Preferred Realities*. New York: W.W. Norton & Company Inc.

Freund, A., & Riediger, M. 2006. Goals as building blocks of personality and development in adulthood. In D.K. Mroczek & T.D. Little (Eds.), *Handbook of Personality Development*. Mahwah, NJ: Erlbaum.

Gapp, S., & Schnell, T. 2008. Intercultural comparison of meaning in life. *International Journal of Psychology*, 43, 3–4, 630.

Grubaugh, A., & Resick, P. A. 2007. Posttraumatic growth in treatment-seeking female assault victims. *Psychiatry Quarterly*, 78, 145–155.

Harper, D., & Moss, D. 2003. A different kind of chemistry? Reformulating formulation. *Clinical Psychology*, 25, 6–10.

Harper, D., & Spellman, D., 2014. Formulation and narrative therapy: Telling a different story. In L. Johnstone & R. Dallos (Eds.), *Formulation in Psychology and Psychotherapy*, 2nd edn. East Sussex: Routledge.

Helgeson, V., Reynolds, K., & Tomich, P. 2006. A meta-analytic review of benefit finding and growth. *Journal of Consulting and Clinical Psychology*, 74, 797–816.

Hermans, H. 2004. The innovation of self-narratives: A dialogical approach. In L. E. Angus & J. MacLeod (Eds.), *The Handbook of Narrative and Psychotherapy*. London: Sage.

Hinkle, D. 1965. *The Change of Personal Constructs from the Viewpoint of a Theory of Construct Implications*. Unpublished PhD thesis. Ohio State University.

Husserl, E. 1960. *Cartesian Meditations: An Introduction to Phenomenology*. The Hague: Nijhoff.

Jacobson, C., Luckhaupt, S., Delaney, S., & Tsevat, J. 2006. Coping, and meaning-making among persons with HIV/AIDS. *Journal for the Scientific Study of Religion*, 45, 1, 39–56.

Johnstone, L., & Dallos, R. 2014. *Formulation in Psychology and Psychotherapy*, 2nd edn. London: Routledge.

Kartalova-O'Doherty, Y., & Tedstone Doherty, D. 2010. *Reconnecting with Life: Personal Experiences of Recovering from Mental Health Problems in Ireland*. Dublin: Health Research Board.

Kelly, G. 1970. A brief introduction to personal construct psychology. In D. Bannister (Ed.), *Perspectives in Personal Construct Psychology*. San Diego: Academic Press.

Kobau, R., Sniezek, J., Zack, M., Lucas, R., & Burns, A. 2010. Wellbeing assessment: An evaluation of wellbeing scales for public health and population estimated of wellbeing among US adults. *Applied Psychology: Health and Wellbeing*, 2, 272–297.

Leitner, L., Faidley, A., & Celentana, M. 2000. Diagnosing human meaning making: An experiential constructivist approach. In R.A. Neimeyer & J.D. Raskin (Eds.), *Constructions of Disorder: Meaning Making Frameworks for Psychotherapy*. Washington, DC: American Psychological Association.

Lodi-Smith, J., Geise, A., Roberts, B., & Robins, R. 2009. Narrating personality change. *Journal of Personality and Social Psychology*, 96, 679–689.

Maddi, S. 1998. Creating meaning through making decisions. In P. Wong & S. Fry (Eds.), *The Human Quest for Meaning: A Handbook of Psychological Research and Clinical Applications*. Mahwah, NJ: Erlbaum.

Marin, K., Bohanek, J., & Fivush, R. 2008. Positive effects of talking about the negative: Family narratives of negative experiences and preadolescents' perceived competence. *Journal of Research on Adolescence*, 18, 573–593.

Mascaro, N., Rosen, D., & Morey, L. 2004. The development, construct validity, and clinical utility of the Spiritual Meaning Scale. *Personality and Individual Differences*, 37, 4, 845–860.

McAdams, D. 2012. Meaning and personality. In P. Wong (Eds.), *The Human Quest for Meaning*. New York: Routledge.

Morgan, A. 2000. *What is Narrative Therapy? An Easy to Read Introduction*. Adelaide: Dulwich Centre Publications.

Morgan, J., & Farsides, T. 2009. Measuring meaning in life. *Journal of Happiness Studies*, 10, 2, 197–214.

Nietzsche, F. 1955. *Beyond Good and Evil*. Chicago, IL: Henry Regnery.

Pals, J., & McAdams, D. 2004. The transformed self: A narrative understanding of posttraumatic growth. *Psychological Inquiry*, 15, 65–69.

Park, C. 2010. Making sense of the meaning literature: An integrative review of meaning making and its effects on adjustment to stressful life events. *Psychological Bulletin*, 136, 257–301.

Park, C. 2013. The meaning making model: A framework for understanding meaning, spirituality, and stress-related growth in health psychology. *The European Health Psychologist*, 15, 2, 40–47.

Park, C., & Folkman, S. 1997. Meaning in the context of stress and coping. *Review of General Psychology*, 1, 115–144.

Payne, M. 2000. *Narrative Therapy: An Introduction for Counselors*. London: Sage Publications.

Plattner, I., & Meiring, N. 2006. Living with HIV: The psychological relevance of meaning making. *AIDS Care*, 18, 3, 241–245.

Procter, H. 2005. Techniques of personal construct family therapy. In D.A. Winter and L. Viney (Eds.), *Personal Construct Psychotherapy: Advances in Theory, Practice and Research*. London: Whurr.

Reese, E., Haden, C., Baker-Ward, L., Bauer, P., Fivush, R., & Ornstein, P. 2011. Coherence in personal narratives: A multidimensional model. *Journal of Cognition and Development*, 12, 1–38.

Rober, P., Elliott, R., Buysse, A., Loots, G., & De Corte, K. 2008. Positioning in the practitioner's inner conversation: A dialogical model based on a grounded theory analysis of practitioner reflections. *Journal of Marital and Family Therapy*, 34, 3, 406–421.

Routledge, C., & Arndt, J. 2009. Creative terror management: Creativity as a facilitator of cultural exploration after mortality salience. *Personality and Social Psychology Bulletin*, 35, 493–505.

Ryan, R., & Deci, E. 2000. Self-determination theory and the facilitation of intrinsic motivation, social development, and wellbeing. *American Psychologist*, 55, 68–78.

Samman, E. 2007. Psychological and subjective wellbeing: A proposal for internationally comparable indicators. *Oxford Development Studies*, 35, 459–486.

Schneider, K., & May, R. 1995. *The Psychology of Existence*. New York: McGraw-Hill.

Schnell, T. 2009. The source of meaning and meaning in life questionnaire (SoMe): Relations to demographics and wellbeing. *Journal of Positive Psychology*, 4, 6, 483–499.

Schnell, T., & Becker, P. 2006. Personality and meaning in life. *Personality and Individual Differences*, 41, 117–129.

Seligman, M. 2011. *Flourish*. New York, NY: Free Press.

Slovic P., Finucane M., Peters E., & MacGregor D. 2002. The affect heuristic. In T. Gilovich, D. Griffin, D. Kahneman (Eds.), *Heuristics and Biases: The Psychology of Intuitive Judgment*. Cambridge, UK: Cambridge Univ. Press.

Spinelli, E. 1989. *The Interpreted World: An Introduction to Phenomenological Psychology*. London: Sage.

Steger, M. 2012. Making meaning in Life. *Psychological Inquiry*, 23, 381–385.

Steger, M., Frazier, P., Oishi, S., & Kaler, M. 2006. The meaning in Life Questionnaire: Assessing the presence of and search for meaning in life. *Journal of Counselling Psychology*, 53, 30–93.

Steger, M., Kashdan, T., & Oishi, S. 2008. Being good by doing good: Daily eudaimonic activity and well-being. *Journal of Research in Personality*, 42, 22–42.

Tedeschi, R., & Calhoun, L. 1996. The posttraumatic growth inventory: Measuring the positive legacy of trauma. *Journal of Traumatic Stress*, 9, 455–471.

Tedeschi, R., & Calhoun, L. 2004. Posttraumatic Growth: Conceptual foundations and empirical evidence. *Psychological Inquiry*, 15, 1–18.

Tschudi, F., & Winter, D. 2011. The ABC model revisited. In P. Caputi, L. Viney, B.M. Walker and N. Crittenden (Eds.), *Personal Construct Methodology*. Chichester: Wiley-Blackwell.

Tversky A., & Kahneman D. 1974. Judgment under uncertainty: Heuristics and biases. *Science*, 185, 1124–1131.

Ugazio, V., Negri, A., & Fellin, L. 2015. Freedom, goodness, power and belonging: The semantics of phobic, obsessive-compulsive, eating and mood disorders. *Journal of Constructivist Psychology*, 28, 4, 293–315.

Van Deurzen, E. 2002. *Existential Counselling and Psychotherapy in Practice*, 2nd edn. London: Sage.

Van Deurzen-Smith, E. 1997. *Everyday Mysteries*. London: Routledge.

Waters, T., Shallcross, J., & Fivush, R. 2013. The many facets of meaning making: Comparing mutiple measures of meaning making and their relations to psychological distress. *Memory*, 21, 1, 111–124.

Watts, M. 2012. Recovery from "mental illness" as a re-enchantment with life: A narrative study. Doctoral thesis, Trinity College Dublin. In S. McDaid., 2013, *Recovery…what should you expect from a good quality mental health service*. Dublin: Mental Health Reform.

White, M. 1991. Deconstruction and therapy. *Dulwich Centre Newsletter*, 3, 21–40.

White, M. 1995. *Externalising Conversations Exercise*. Adelaide: Dulwich Centre Publications.

White, M., & Epston, D. 1990. *Narrative Means to the Therapeutic Ends*. New York: Norton.

Williams, E., Polster, D., Grizzard, B., Rockenbaugh, J., & Judge, A. 2003. What happens when practitioners feel bored or anxious: A qualitative study of distracting self-awareness and practitioners' management strategies. *Journal of Contemporary Psychotherapy*, 33, 5–18.

Wong, P. 1998. Implicit theories of meaningful life and the development of the Personal Meaning Profile (PMP). In P. Wong & P. Fry (Eds.), *The Human Quest for Meaning: A Handbook for Psychological Research and Clinical Applications*. Mahwah, NJ: Erlbaum.

Wong, P. 2012. Towards a dual systems model of what makes life worth living. In P. Wong (Eds.), *The Human Quest for Meaning: Theories, Research and Applications*. New York: Routledge.

Yalom, I. 1980. *Existential Psychotherapy*. New York, NY: Basic Books.

Zoellner, T., & Maercker, A. 2006. Posttraumatic growth in clinical psychology—A critical review and introduction of a two component model. *Clinical Psychology Review*, 26, 5, 626–653.

Chapter 3

Integrating neuroscience in formulation

Patrick Ryan, Fergal Connolly, and Rory Carolan

CHAPTER TOPICS

- Review of general neuroscience principles that can underpin formulation
- How neuroscience can aid our understanding of common cognitive deficits in clients attending mental health services
- The synthesis of neuroscience into formulation approaches
- Potential barriers in integrating neuroscience into formulation

Introduction

Formulation is a key competency for mental health practitioners, forming the link between the assessment and treatment planning processes (Restifo 2010). Bieling and Kuyken (2003) argued that an accurate formulation will have an impact on treatment outcome, either via the selection of appropriate interventions, or through enhancing the therapeutic relationship. Practitioners typically adopt one theoretical framework within which to formulate; however in recent years, efforts have been made to develop integrative formulation approaches that incorporate information from a wide range of therapeutic perspectives, to enhance the impact of formulation on intervention.

Formulation has comparatively less attention in the literature compared to diagnosis. A recent systematic review explored the reliability of case formulation, particularly in relation to its fidelity to the scientist-practitioner model (Flinn et al. 2015). This systematic review found varied inter-rater reliability for case formulations based on mental health presentations. The challenge to reliability within this population is potentially due to the heterogeneity of mental health presentations. For example, there can be significant discrepancies between individual clinical presentations of depression: That is, a client who presents with low mood and irritability will be characterised as presenting with depression, the same as a client presenting with persistent low mood. Another way of interpreting these findings, is to recognise that inter-rater reliabilities are going to be confounded by therapist orientation; psychodynamic formulations were linked with improved levels of reliability over cognitive or behavioural formulations. The assessment process provides vast quantities of material with which the therapist must prioritise and synthesise based on how they perceive psychological health and distress. This practitioner variation, while presenting a barrier to the reliability and validity of formulation could be considered a strength in terms of service provision, as long as the formulation has ecological validity on an individual level (Flinn et al. 2015).

In an effort to make formulations more ecologically valid, research has highlighted a number of common factors in mental health illness that should be incorporated into a mental health formulation, irrespective of theoretical orientation. These include coping skills, decision-making capacity, insight, sense of identity, unprocessed trauma, and disturbed interpersonal attachments (Restifo 2010).

Further research has advocated a transdiagnostic perspective on mental health, moving away from specific diagnoses and more towards examining the common processes that prevail in mental illness onset and maintenance. Garland and Howard's (2014) article suggests a transdiagnostic perspective to investigate the explanatory role of automacity, attentional bias, memory bias, interpretation bias, and thought suppression in psychosocial distress formation (Garland and Howard 2014).

Neuroscience has been one of the fastest growing research paradigms in the field of mental health and illness in recent years. Research has examined the role that genes, proteins, neurotransmitters, and structural, functional, and interconnectivity abnormalities within the brain play in mental health illness development and maintenance. This chapter examines the utility of incorporating a neuroscience perspective into case formulation within mental health practice. The chapter pays particular attention to schizophrenia and explores how neuroscience research has enriched our understanding of the precipitating and perpetuating factors associated with this presenting problem. While neuroscience is useful at describing factors associated with psychological distress, it does not, on its own, meet scientific criteria in terms of providing an explanatory account for such distress. The maximal utility of such findings is through its synthesis with other aspects of the assessment process. Discussion on how to incorporate these findings within a case formulation will be outlined later, before the implications of such synthesis within professional practice are discussed.

Modern day mental health practice is challenged with balancing the demands of utilising evidence-based theoretical frameworks that account for the aetiology of a mental health presentation, while creating the space necessary to incorporate qualitatively different individual factors and experiences each individual possesses (Shapiro 2014). This chapter will highlight that it is not a person's genetic makeup, or the events that they have been through that precipitates mental health problems but rather that these are dependent on the complex interplay among genetics, environmental factors, and the meaning that a person attaches to a particular set of experiences or a general way of being.

The chapter sets out to examine what role neuroscience could play in the formulation process for people with mental health disorders experiencing psychological distress. Rather than considering it as a novel theoretical perspective from which to examine distress, it is proposed that adding a neuroscience perspective to the health-illness continuum will enhance formulation, intervention, and symptom resolution. As the field of neuroscience is so vast, a brief introduction to neuroscience is provided, before a summary of recent literature in the field of schizophrenia is explored through the lens of a neuroscience perspective, with a focus on the role of the hippocampal region in working memory impairment, and social dysfunction in people with schizophrenia. Brief mention will also be made of neuroscientific findings associated with other mental health difficulties, including depression, anxiety, and bipolar disorder.

Relevance of neuroscience principles to formulation

The development and modernisation of brain imaging technology has been successful in localising specific functions associated with particular brain regions. Studies have also uncovered a greater understanding of the role of neurotransmitters and proteins in typical and atypical brain functioning (Yudofsky and Hales 2004). While particular neurotransmitters have been implicated in specific psychiatric diagnoses, it has not been proven that such illnesses are solely attributable to these chemical imbalances (Valenstein 1998). Long-term prospective studies have shown that people are most likely to develop mental disorders when they are genetically vulnerable and experience stressful life events (Caspi et al. 2002, 2003).

The brain remains the most complicated observable and measurable system in the universe (Basar and Karakas 2006). While historically the brain was conceptualised as a fairly static and stable organ (Leuner and Gould 2010), there is now a growing acceptance that the brain is a dynamic entity, capable of change particularly in the context of learning and memory (Kays et al. 2012). Recent neuroscientific advances have highlighted the discovery of neurogenesis in the adult human brain (Curtis et al. 2011; Landgren and Curtis 2011). The term neuroplasticity has been used to describe changes within the dynamic brain that are attributable to a range of internal, external, and combined factors (Kerr et al. 2011). Neuroplasticity can involve the formation of new neurons and glial cells (neurogenesis), as well as the formation of new connections and alterations in existing ones through multiple processes such as synapse formation, axonal sprouting, and pruning (Kays et al. 2012). Such changes can be conceptualised as either adaptive or maladaptive. Exposure to chronic stress, depression, and physical illness are all factors that have been linked to suppressed neurogenesis (Wosiski-Kuhn and Stranahan 2012; Schoenfeld and Gould 2012).

The human brain is a complex, adaptive, self-organising system arranged in parallel distributed neural networks. In the brain, functional differentiation is coupled with flexible integration of neuronal components, and continually changing patterns of activity compete for access to consciousness (Edelman 2004). Primary neural networks are a basic property of any living system – monitoring the immediate environment and enabling reflexive action. Secondary neural networks monitor changes in the primary neural networks following an environmental exchange. They account for primary consciousness such as pain awareness in response to an aversive stimulus. Tertiary networks monitor changes in the secondary networks over time, allowing for reflective consciousness, which is the metacognitive skill of awareness of being aware. Unique human capabilities like insight, emotional awareness, free will, and meaning are associated with tertiary networks. They are based in the higher associative cortical areas that integrate sensory, interoceptive and emotional information, such as cingulate, profrontal/orbitofrontal, and temporo-parietal cortices (Lieberman 2007).

Imaging studies of human brains have indicated changes that occur through learning. Engaging in task practice leads to significant increase in cortical representation for muscle groups involved, suggesting increased neural connections to support task performance (Kays et al. 2012). Such increased activity has also been found on mental tasks, such as visualising task completion, suggesting that visualisation and other mental rehearsal strategies can produce neuroplastic changes in the brain. The challenge for practitioners is to harness neuroplasticity to promote healing and recovery. Brain plasticity may play a key role in individual coping and adjustment to stress and mental illness (DeCarolis and Eisch 2010).

Developments in neuroimaging capabilities have facilitated significant research and findings into the functional capabilities of a wide range of brain regions (Basar and Karakas 2006). The human brain, with its connections of billions of neurons, demonstrates remarkable synchronicity on a whole-brain level, while also demonstrating synchronicity within specific brain structures (Bressler and Tognoli 2006).

One of the pioneering researchers into learning and memory was Lashley (1929), who attempted to identify specific brain regions in which memories were stored. While his research on rats failed to identify specific locations in which memory was stored, he did generate his concept of equipotentiality -- where memories are stored over the whole brain region. Similarly, Hebb (1949) developed the key concept of co-operativity, a viewpoint that proposes that neurons that fire together tend to become strengthened together as a unit, which ultimately developed as a key tenet of neuroscience.

It has been argued that consciousness and attention are key processes that facilitate learning (Grossberg 1999). Attention can be described as a conscious attempt to apportion available cognitive resources to an event (Hahn et al. 2006). Attention has also been described as a selective capacity, either under voluntary control or driven by a stimulus. Research highlights that automatic attentional selection occurs if stimuli are intense, dynamic, or biologically or personally important (Hahn et al. 2006). The voluntary control of attention is attributed to the prefrontal cortex (Klingberg, Forssberg and Westerberg 2002). Synchronisation of frontal and parietal brain regions have been shown to enable flexible control of voluntary attention (Baars 2005).

In terms of clinical relevance, when an individual presents in a mental health clinic for the first time it is useful to explore their current conscious awareness.

The mini mental status exam (Folstein 1975) enables practitioners to investigate the cognitive status of the patient for the clinician's benefit (McDougall 1990). The mini mental status exam involves the following components: orientation to person, place, time; brief working memory task; attention and mental manipulation; immediate recall; language (naming common objects); visuomotor capabilities (replication of a line drawing). The components of the mini mental status exam all involve voluntary control and conscious direction of attention. People with frontal lobe deficits experience difficulties in these tasks due to executive dysfunction. Performance can also be impaired by drowsiness, inattention, and the influence of prescribed medication.

Learning and memory are evolutionary functions that facilitate flexible adaptation to our surrounding environment (Baars and Gage 2010). It has been argued that memory could be conceptualised as a distributed property of various cortical systems, with communication and cooperation between these brain regions vital in facilitating memory encoding, storage, consolidation, and retrieval (Bressler and Togoli 2006). Seitz and Watanabe (2005) proposed that declarative and episodic learning occurs via the direction of attention to novel information that becomes conscious. This information is then processed and stored for future retrieval.

The temporal lobe has traditionally been associated with memory function (Squire and Zola-Morgan 1991). Current conceptualisation of memory and learning proposes that the medial temporal lobes play a key role in the storage and retrieval of daily life experiences, with a particular role for the hippocampus. The hippocampus combines information from cognitive and emotional brain areas, binding that synthesised information into a memory trace that codes for all experiences of a consciously experienced event (Moscovitch 1995). The medial temporal lobes are highly connected with other brain regions, integrating information on multiple levels from multiple sources, including visual information, auditory information, and olfactory inputs. The amygdala is located close to the hippocampus and is also associated with particular aspects of memory formation, particularly fear conditioning (LeDoux 1996).

Neuroscience and mental health

Neuroscience has been hypothesised as the missing link between the identification of specific biomarkers for mental disorders and facilitating a greater understanding of the aetiology of mental illness. These biomarkers could take the form of particular genes, proteins, neurotransmitters, or specific brain regions implicated in particular forms of mental illness. Neuroscience has certainly added to our understanding of the brain and its functions; however, it has not revolutionised mental health service provision. It has not led to the development of novel, target treatments. Nor has it provided an explanatory account of any mental health illness. Such aims are, potentially, inherently flawed and while such aspirations persist, maximal use of neuroscience information will not occur (Paris 2013).

Clinical experience has shown that individuals can never be characterised by a unitary perspective. No single biological, psychological, interpersonal, systemic, or contextual factor can account for the development and maintenance of mental health difficulties. It is an inherently reductionist view which, if adopted, would ignore the role of a range of interacting factors in mental health aetiology. The key role that neuroscience may play in informing our understanding of mental health is to show how such factors integrate and combine to generate the symptoms that are described by clients who experience mental health distress.

Neuroscience and social dysfunction in schizophrenia

Commonly encountered difficulties among individuals with schizophrenia include problematic interpersonal relationships, social dysfunction, and social isolation (Fett et al. 2015). This occurs in spite of the fact that social performance is typically normal prior to illness onset, which usually commences in late adolescence or early adulthood. Research has proposed that such difficulties with social interactions are mediated by deficits in social cognitive information processing, positing social dysfunction as a prominent maintenance factor in schizophrenia (Fett et al. 2011). Social cognition explores information processing within social-emotional contexts (Fett et al. 2015). It is necessary for conquering the tasks associated with social interaction, such as recognition of social stimuli, interpersonal cues, and identification of appropriate social behaviour in a particular context.

Emotional recognition is considered one of the pillars of social neuroscience. It is fundamental in the recognition of the affective signals of others. Emotion recognition has been widely researched in schizophrenia both on a behavioural and neuroimaging level. Behavioural experiments have highlighted significant deficits that are particularly pronounced for the recognition of negative emotions (Hoekert et al. 2007). Such deficits have been found across all stages of illness; however, these deficits deteriorate during acute illness phases (Kohler et al. 2010). Neuroimaging studies in relation to emotion recognition in schizophrenia have highlighted decreased activation in the bilateral parahippocampal gyrus, amygdala, right superior frontal gyrus, and middle occipital gyrus (Li et al. 2010). Additional research has identified decreased activation in the right ventral lateral prefrontal cortex and posterior cingulate, left amygdala, right occipito-temporal regions including the fusiform gyrus and the left thalamus (Sugranyes et al. 2011). Decreased activation in the occipital regions associated with early visual processing such as the anterior cingulate cortex, the dorsal lateral prefrontal cortex, and subcortical areas such as the thalamus, caudate, and midbrain have also been noted (Taylor et al. 2012).

Theory of mind is another core feature of social functioning consistently impaired in individuals with schizophrenia (Sprong et al. 2007). This has been explored using behavioural tasks such as the interpretation of the mental state of characters in vignettes. Neuroimaging research has highlighted lower activation in the medial prefrontal cortex, temporal cortices and the right posterior cingulate in patients with schizophrenia (Sugranyes et al. 2011). Research has also identified increased activation in the inferior parietal lobule, inferior frontal gyrus, precuneus, and cerebellum (Pedersen et al. 2012). Research on theory of mind in people with paranoid subtype of schizophrenia has shown that excessive interpretation of the behaviour and intentions of others as malevolent and self-referent is common (Frith 2004). Imaging studies have shown that positive symptoms of schizophrenia were related to overmentalising theory of mind errors while negative symptoms appears related more to a lack of theory of mind (Montag et al. 2011).

The third aspect of social dysfunction for noting is empathy. Behavioural, cognitive, and affective empathy has been examined by getting people to watch or read about physical or social pain in other people (Jackson, Meltzoff, and Decety 2005) or, more recently, using the Questionnaire of Cognitive and Affective Empathy (QCAE) (Horan, Reise, Kern, Lee, Penn and Green 2015). Alternatively, studies have examined empathy by getting people to observe facial expressions of negative emotions and to judge the emotional state of themselves and others (Fett et al. 2015). Among people with schizophrenia, empathy has typically been explored via the administration of self-report questionnaires on trait empathy. The most enduring finding within such research domains has been higher personal distress when others are in difficult situations (Lee et al. 2011). Other studies have found lower self-reported empathic concern (Smith et al. 2012). Neuroimaging studies have suggested a reduced neural response across cortical and subcortical areas in response to affective stimuli (Harvey et al. 2013). This reduced response appears in some way linked to reduced activation in brain regions on tasks relating to emotion recognition and theory of mind.

A lack of trust and motivation to engage in prosocial behaviour have been found in studies examining schizophrenia, theory of mind, and dopamine deficits adopting a turn-taking shared output task (Fett et al. 2015). Such a lack of trust remained in spite of explicit instruction that the co-participant was trustworthy. This reduced trust has been linked to decreased activation in the caudate (Gromann et al. 2013). Decreased activation in the caudate has also been associated with increased paranoia. Such social trust issues reduce the likelihood of people with schizophrenia experiencing benefits from social interaction and could have radical implications for treatment planning: that is this may inhibit the development of a healthy collaborative therapeutic relationship between clinician and client. It could also contribute to the maintenance of social impairment through the course of illness (Eisenberger and Cole 2012).

KEY POINT

Clients with schizophrenia have been shown to have reduced trust and motivation compared to the general population; this finding may have implications for the development of a therapeutic alliance, service engagement and the efficacy of social prescribing.

The hippocampus, schizophrenia, and memory deficits

Research on people with schizophrenia has highlighted deficits in working memory and declarative memory when compared to non-schizophrenia controls (Wible 2013). The hippocampus has been postulated as an area that processes and integrates information and is active during tasks relating to working memory (Hannula et al. 2006). Schizophrenia has long been considered to have a genetic component, with age of illness onset typically occurring in adolescence or early adulthood (Feinberg 1982). Studies have highlighted brain abnormalities at time of illness onset and a higher incidence rate in males than females (Jablensky 2000).

Both learning and memory are significantly impaired in schizophrenia. Impaired declarative verbal memory has been consistently reported in clients with schizophrenia (Cirillo and Seidman 2003). This deficit in impaired declarative verbal memory has been found to be stable over time and is considered independent of other functions like verbal fluency (Wible 2013).

The hippocampus and surrounding structures have been implicated in declarative memory functioning (Wible et al. 1997). Evidence for this has been found in studies that have highlighted decreased hippocampal volume and hippocampal hyperactivity among people with schizophrenia (Elliott et al. 2009). The role of this hyperactivity in the positive and negative symptoms of schizophrenia continues to be examined, with research identifying hippocampal hyperactivity prior to and during auditory hallucinations (Diederen et al. 2010).

The hippocampus is a highly connected structure capable of significant neuroplasticity (Cohen et al. 1999). It is linked with higher order perceptual regions where long-term memory is eventually stored. Its function in the declarative memory process is in synthesising multiple inputs from various modalities to facilitate the storage of representations of the associations among the constituent elements involved in the inputs (Cohen et al. 1999). Such representations can then be stored in long-term memory structures distributed across higher order cortical regions. Communication between the hippocampus and various cortical regions is facilitated by interconnections within the medial temporal lobe, collectively referred to as the hippocampal system (composed of dentate gyrus, cornu ammonis (CA1–4) fields, and subiculum). Due to the high levels of interconnection between the hippocampus, medial temporal lobe, and adjacent cortical structures, hyperactivation of the hippocampus has a knock-on effect on functioning within connected cortical structures (Cohen et al. 1999). Information flows from various cortical regions into the hippocampus, and back out again in a continuous feedback loop, enabling formation, storage and retrieval of memories, facilitated by high levels of neuroplasticity within the hippocampal system throughout the lifetime (Epp et al. 2013).

The temporal parietal junction has received significant attention in the literature due to its high interconnectivity with the hippocampal system (Kahn et al. 2008). Deficits in this region have been linked to working memory deficits present in individuals with schizophrenia (Wible 2013), in contrast with previous hypotheses that impairments in working memory in schizophrenia were linked to frontal lobe dysfunction (Lee and Park 2005). A potential mechanism to account for this has been the evidence that excitotoxic hyperactivation of the hippocampus leads to hyperactivity in the temporal parietal junction which has been shown to lead to memory deficits (Wible 2012).

Research has shown that the subiculum experiences significantly increase in myelination during late adolescence, which has been identified as the typical stage of onset of schizophrenia (Benes 1989). Studies have highlighted how male hippocampal volume increases significantly during late adolescence, possibly accounting for the increased incidence of schizophrenia among males compared to females (Suzuki et al. 2005).

Neuroscience and additional mental health presentations

Neuroscience research has also examined its potential influence in the aetiology and presentation in other mental health conditions. Individuals with depression exhibit a thinking style that is predominantly negative, particularly in relation to the self (Whisman et al. 1993). Depression also has a distinct cognitive profile (Steer et al. 1994). Individuals with depression exhibit a processing bias for negative self-referent information (Moretti et al. 1996). On an anatomical level, impairment in emotional functioning and regulation have been linked to anomalies in structure, function, and connectivity in associated brain regions (Hamilton et al. 2013; Singh and Gotlib 2014). Such regions implicated include the amygdala and hippocampus (Sacher et al. 2012), ventral striatum and dorsolateral prefrontal cortex (Hamitlon et al. 2012).

KEY POINT

Neuroscience insights may help practitioners to engender a greater appreciation of the genesis and presentation of depression; liaising with neuropsychology may help practitioners to formulate a more accurate timeline of the disease lifespan of depression and clients' likelihood to respond to pharmacological and/or psychotherapy intervention.

Bipolar disorder can have a heterogeneous presentation due to the multiple combinations of symptoms and duration of episodes (Sala et al. 2009). Neuroscience research into bipolar disorder has identified the following deficits: Emotion processing, executive function, attention, impulse control, working memory, reward and risk response, perspective taking, and interface of emotion and cognition (Pavuluri 2015). Imaging findings in the field have identified prefrontal cortex improvement structurally and functionally in response to pharmacological treatment (longer-term treatment is typically required for improvement in amygdala functioning). Impaired emotion processing findings include excessive reactivity to negative emotions, impaired face emotion recognition, and missing subtle cues (West et al. 2014). Executive dysfunction difficulties have been demonstrated in the areas of cognitive inflexibility, poor problem solving, poor forward planning and shifting, poor verbal detail (Passarotti 2014). Impulsivity manifests in impaired ability to control responses and to accurately time the responses. Reward and risk processing includes: excitability with rewards, frustration with losses, and inability to wait for reward. Inattention includes: sustained attention problems and biased attention to negative cues. Perspective taking deficits include: inability to grasp hints, especially in the context of negative stories. Working memory deficits include: an inability to remember numbers or words, especially if complex or multiple steps are involved in learning and remembering verbal information (Pavuluri 2014). Impairment at the interface of emotion and cognition includes cognitive deficits that occur in the context of intense emotions, particularly intense negative emotions (Sala et al. 2009). The cognitive difficulties mentioned above (attention, working memory, verbal memory, and executive function) persist in between depressive episodes and worsen with age, particularly if untreated (Pavuluri 2015).

KEY POINT

Cognitive deficits commonly experienced among clients with mental illness include poor executive function, impulsivity, working memory deficits and emotional recognition and experienced emotion: A holistic formulation must take into account these cognitive deficits and neurological damage when evaluating suitability for treatments and treatment outcomes for patients.

Research into the neuroscience of anxiety disorders has shown the involvement of specific brain regions in the development of maladaptive fear responses (Kindt 2014). The amygdala, hippocampus, and ventromedial prefrontal cortex have all been implicated in anxiety disorders (Visser et al. 2013), as has the role of stress hormones within the hippocampus, amygdala, and prefrontal cortex in maladaptive fear generalisation (Krugers et al. 2011). The role of cortisol within the basolateral amygdala has also been implicated in maladaptive fear contextualisation (Kaouane et al. 2012).

Synthesis of neuroscience into case formulation approaches

Cognitive behavioural therapy is one of the most widely used therapeutic modalities in clinical psychology practice (Bieling and Kuyken 2003). Adopting a cognitive-behavioural case conceptualisation approach to formulation has proven effective in the treatment of depression and various anxiety disorders (Persons 2008). Case conceptualisation provides a framework through which to describe an individual's presenting problem, with context provided in relation to factors that precipitated and perpetuate the problem. Ideally, a case formulation is reliable and valid and enables practitioners to select interventions grounded in theory and that have an empirically validated evidence base (Eells 1997). Insight and self- awareness are key factors to consider in a case conceptualisation, both of which have been shown to be impaired in individuals with mental health difficulties, particularly those in chronic phases of illness trajectory. Given that one current predominant research paradigm is cognitive neuroscience, it is proposed that incorporating neuroscientific research findings will enrich a cognitive behavioural case formulation in mental health. For example, recognising that people with schizophrenia have difficulties in relation to working memory and social functioning, and that particular brain regions have structural and functional abnormalities as a result, can lead to treatment planning that promotes recovery and well-being. Co-ordinated service provision on a multidisciplinary team basis can ensure that pharmacological intervention targeting changes on a neural level can be complemented with psychotherapeutic intervention targeting social deficits, memory deficits, and other difficulties encountered in schizophrenia.

KEY POINT

The recognition of cognitive deficits and impaired executive functioning as a result of structural and/or functional abnormalities and its relation to behavioural outcomes may require a multidisciplinary approach to ensure a comprehensive formulation.

The neuroscience perspective to psychodynamic formulation hypothesises that subjective experiences and memory are encoded in the dynamic patterns of cortical synaptic network activity – giving the uniqueness of human experience a complexity far in excess of what our minds can calculate (Shapiro 2014). Practitioners from a psychodynamic orientation explore developmental and relational patterns that may have predisposed an individual to develop psychiatric illness, precipitated its onset, and perpetuate its course. Such patterns may be evident on the behavioural level or may also become apparent through exploring the person's subjective meaning and emotional experience of the events they have experienced. People are not passive recipients of life events – they actively construct meaning out of their experiences. The human brain uses heuristics and biases as shortcuts to making decisions. Psychodynamic practitioners aim to bring such heuristics to the level of conscious awareness to enable the person to change such dysfunctional patterns of decision making if in fact they are deemed dysfunctional (Shapiro 2014).

Shapiro (2014) described a three-dimensional 'map of the mind', with peaks and valleys for likes and dislikes, and various networks of typical decision-making processes that predict our life choices based on typical circumstances. He describes this map as dynamic and amenable to change with conscious effort. He considers the *first challenge* when working with a person is to identify patterns of thinking, feeling, and relating that represent the typical response style based on the person's unique synaptic network configuration encoding their life experiences. Specific areas to explore in this section would be: (a) patterns of experiencing self-in-the-world (mastery vs. inadequacy); (b) patterns of experiencing self-with-others (intimacy vs. isolation); (c) patterns of self-experience (meaning vs. despair). Fundamentally: what is the pattern, and why does it continue to occur? Interjections like *'is this a familiar place for you?'* may help to explore this further with the client. A person internalises their subjective experiences. This internalisation leads to specific synaptic modifications that shape a person's information processing style, thus perpetuating the likelihood that future experiences are subjectively internalised in a similar fashion.

In Shapiro's (2014) proposed framework, the *second challenge* is to consider the person's patterns and symptoms as manifestations of their adaptations to the adversities they have encountered in their developmental environment. These can be inherited (genetic), environmental, or a product of gene-environment interactions. Specific markers in this area include: temperamental predispositions; biological vulnerabilities; family history (genetics); family of origin environment, relational experiences, developmental trauma, cultural background and beliefs (environment); identification of the central dynamic theme (gene-environment interaction). Within Shapiro's approach, the third stage involves identifying why the individual is choosing (consciously or unconsciously) to maintain dysfunctional patterns today. Areas to explore include: what are the key choices contributing to the current problem? What predisposed the person to react this way? What meaning do they attribute to their choices? Why are you looking for help now? Therapists are not passive listeners but active participants in patient experience.

KEY POINT

Shapiro's three-dimensional 'map of the mind' may help to formulate a greater understanding of the aetiology of a client's mental illness along both biological/genetic lines and cognitive decision-making patterns which may maintain maladaptive outcomes.

The current prevailing paradigm in mainstream psychology and psychotherapy practice is the adoption of an integrative approach to formulation (Johnstone and Dallos 2006, 2013). This approach promotes the utilisation of a wide range of therapeutic orientations on an individual and systemic level to develop detailed formulations in relation to understanding the development and maintenance of psychological difficulties.

Neuroscience has a significant role to play in aiding our understanding of these illnesses by further enabling practitioners to tailor their approach when working with clients. For example, if working with an individual with schizophrenia, an awareness that working memory impairments are common will enable the practitioner to tailor their verbal communication approach with the client accordingly. Similarly, maintaining an awareness of the social dysfunction typically encountered will enable the practitioner to acknowledge that there may be difficulties in relation to trust in the therapist and the therapy process. Such trust difficulties may provide a barrier to the establishment of a healthy therapeutic relationship; however, a skilled practitioner mindful of this will be able to pay the required attention to the fostering of a safe, trusting therapeutic relationship (McCabe et al. 2012). The therapeutic relationship has long been considered the key common factor across all therapies and research investigating the neuroscience underpinning this relationship, particularly impairments identified through neuroscience research, could enable practitioners to more effectively establish therapeutic rapports with clients, and thus increase the likelihood of positive outcomes in therapy.

KEY POINT

Neuroscience has the potential to aid formulation in a number of ways: (a) identify suitable pharmacological interventions for clients with anomalies in brain structure and (b) allow practitioners to tailor their approach with clients who may struggle to form trusting therapeutic relationships and lasting attachment.

Implications for practice

Neuroscience is already contributing greatly to the field of mental health practice. Research has shown the benefit of incorporating a neuroscientific perspective into psychiatry training programmes in the United States, with an explicit focus on encouraging the integration of neuroscience information into case formulations in inpatient mental health settings (Posner et al. 2007). While this research focused on a single training programme, the case-study style write-up clearly highlighted the benefit that information from a neuroscience perspective added to case understanding, particularly in relation to illness description from a biological perspective. This focus on biological descriptions via structural or functional brain imaging, neurotransmitter deficits, or the role of specific genes or proteins in mental health remains at best descriptive. It is not definitive, and as mentioned previously there continues to be no specific biomarkers identified in relation to specific mental health diagnoses. However, despite the lack of specificity or definitive nature of such associations, an awareness of this information clearly enriches case formulation and guides interventions. Just like any other aspect of a case formulation, that is, systemic factors, contextual factors, or psychological factors, neuroscience brings specific information to our understanding of mental distress that when added to other data, broadens comprehension of presenting problems in a manner that can improve decision making pertaining to intervention.

KEY POINT

Neuroscience can add value to the formulation process by introducing a biological suggestion for progression and presentation of mental illness that may not be explained by social or contextual factors.

As flexible practitioners that adopt various theoretical orientations depending on the unique characteristics of a given case, mental health professionals should be able to take the useful aspects of neuroscience literature in the field of mental health and integrate this into their case formulation. The challenge as always will be how best to prioritise the volume of information obtained via assessment, not only neuroscientific information, but the intrapersonal, interpersonal, and contextual factors at play. Given the heterogeneous presentation of mental health conditions, it is probable that two cases of a specific disorder will not mirror each other. While there are commonalities, and typical factors present, their expression within a given service is unique to each individual. Again, the idea of meaning making comes to mind. The double hermeneutic tradition of psychotherapy, where the therapist makes sense of the client's attempts at making sense of their experiences, appears to hold the key to understanding why mental health difficulties present so differently in the clinic setting (Barclay 1992).

KEY POINT

The heterogeneity of patients attending mental health services reiterates the need for practitioners to identify stable characteristics of mental health presentation to increase validity of formulation; neuroscientific input may improve the ecological validity of clinical formulation and suitability for treatment.

Such a perspective fits with that proposed by Eells (2013) who wrote of the importance of developing an evidence-based case formulation approach to psychotherapy. Such a perspective has greater structure than solely trusting clinical judgement and intuition; however, it also provides greater flexibility than rigidly adhering to manualised empirically supported treatments, with practitioners able to select a framework under which to operate once that framework is empirically validated.

In terms of neuroscience, such findings would in fact have that empirical basis and would be amenable to integration into evidence-based case formulation approaches.

Conclusion

Neuroscience has a key role to play in increasing our understanding of mental illness. It cannot solely account for why some people develop mental health difficulties and others do not. It is unlikely that any sole factor will ever be able to adequately account for why psychological distress occurs. However, an understanding of the neuroscience of mental health difficulties can be of great benefit to practitioners in formulation. While neuroscience is a factor difficult to explore on a conversational basis with a client, interdisciplinary communication and the utilisation of neuroimaging information around brain structure, function, and connectivity can vastly increase a practitioner's understanding of psychological disorder on an individual basis.

REFERENCES

Baars, B.J. 2005. Global workspace theory of consciousness: Toward a cognitive neuroscience of human experience. *Progress in Brain Research*, 150, 45–53.

Baars, B.J., & Gage, N.M. 2010. *Cognition, Brain, and Consciousness: Introduction to Cognitive Neuroscience*. Academic Press.

Barclay, M.W. 1992. The utility of hermeneutic interpretation in psychotherapy. *Theoretical & Philosophical Psychology*, 12(2), 103.

Basar, E., & Karakas, S. 2006. Neuroscience is awaiting for a breakthrough: A chapter bridging the concepts of Descartes, Einstein, Heisenberg, Hebb and Hayek with the explanatory formulations in this special issue. *International Journal of Psychophysiology*, 60, 194–201.

Benes, F. 1989. Myelination of cortical-hippocampal relays during late adolescence. *Schizophrenia Bulletin*, 15(4), 585–593.

Bieling, P., & Kuyken, W. 2003. Is cognitive case formulation science or science fiction? *Clinical Psychology: Science and Practice*, 10(1), 52–69.

Bressler, S., & Tognoli, E. 2006. Operational principles of neurocognitive networks. *International Journal of Psychophysiology*, 60, 139–148.

Caspi, A., McClay, J., Moffitt, T.E., Mill, J., Martin, J., Craig, I.W., Taylor, A. & Poulton, R. 2002. Role of genotype in the cycle of violence in maltreated children. *Science*, 297(5582), 851–854.

Caspi, A., Sugden, K., Moffitt, T.E., Taylor, A., Craig, I.W., Harrington, H. et al. 2003. Influence of life stress on depression: moderation by a polymorphism in the 5-HTT gene. *Science*, 301(5631), 386–389.

Cirillo, M., & Seidman, L. 2003. Verbal declarative memory dysfunction in schizophrenia: From clinical assessment to genetics and brain mechanisms. *Neuropsychology Review*, 13(2), 43–77.

Cohen, N., Ryan, J., Hunt, C., Romine, L., Wszalek, T., & Nash, C. 1999. Hippocampal system and declarative (relational) memory: Summarizing the data from functional neuroimaging studies. *Hippocampus*, 9(1), 83–98.

Curtis, M.A., Kam, M., & Faull, R.L. 2011. Neurogenesis in humans. *European Journal of Neuroscience*, 33(6), 1170–1174.

DeCarolis, N.A., & Eisch, A.J. 2010. Hippocampal neurogenesis as a target for the treatment of mental illness: A critical evaluation. *Neuropharmacology*, 58(6), 884–893.

Diederen, K., Neggers, S., Daalman, K., Blom, J., Goekoop, R., Kahn, R., & Sommer, I. 2010. Deactivation of the parahippocampal gyrus preceding auditory hallucinations in schizophrenia. *American Journal of Psychiatry*, 167(4), 427–435.

Edelman, G.M. 2004. *Wider than the Sky: The Phenomenal Gift of Consciousness.* Yale University Press.

Eells, T. 1997. *Handbook of Psychotherapy Case Formulation.* New York: Guildford Press.

Eells, T. 2013. In support of evidence-based case formulation in psychotherapy (from the perspective of a clinician). *Pragmatic Case Studies in Psychotherapy*, 4(5), 457–467.

Eisenberger, N., & Cole, S. 2012. Social neuroscience and health: Neurophysiological mechanisms linking social ties with physical health. *Nature Neuroscience*, 15(5), 669–674.

Elliott, B., Joyce, E., & Shorvon, S. 2009. Delusions, illusions and hallucinations in epilepsy: 2. *Complex Phenomena and Psychosis, Epilepsy Research*, 85(2/3), 172–186.

Epp, J., Chow, C., & Galea, L. 2013. Hippocampus-dependent learning influences hippocampal neurogenesis. *Frontiers in Evolutionary Neuroscience*, 7, 1–9.

Feinberg, I. 1982. Schizophrenia: Caused by a fault in programmed synaptic elimination during adolescence? *Journal of Psychiatric Research*, 17(4), 319–334.

Fett, A., Shergill, S., & Krabbendam, L. 2015. Social neuroscience in psychiatry: Unravelling the neural mechanisms of social dysfunction. *Psychological Medicine*, 45(6), 1145–1165.

Fett, A., Viechtbauer, W., Dominguez, M., Penn, D., van Os, J., & Krabbendam, L. 2011 The relationship between neurocognition and social cognition with functional outcomes in schizophrenia: A meta-analysis. *Neuroscience and Biobehavioral Reviews*, 35(3), 573–588.

Flinn, L., Braham, L., & dasNair, R. 2015. How reliable are case formulations? A systematic literature review. *British Journal of Clinical Psychology*, 54, 266–290.

Folstein, M.E. 1975. A practical method for grading the cognitive state of patients for the children. *Journal of Psychiatric Research*, 12, 189–198.

Frith, C.D. 2004. Schizophrenia and theory of mind. *Psychological Medicine*, 34(3), 385–389.

Garland, E., & Howard, M. 2014 A transdiagnostic perspective on cognitive, affective and neurobiological processes underlying human suffering. *Research on Social Work Practice*, 24(1), 142–151.

Gromann, P., Heslenfeld, D., Fett, A., Joyce, D., Shergill, S., & Krabbendam, L. 2013. Trust versus paranoia: Abnormal response to social reward in psychotic illness. *Brain: A Journal of Neurology*, 136(6), 1968–1975.

Grossberg, S. 1999. The link between brain learning, attention, and consciousness. *Consciousness and Cognition*, 8(1), 1–44.

Hahn, B., Ross, T.J. & Stein, E.A. 2006. Cingulate activation increases dynamically with response speed under stimulus unpredictability. *Cerebral Cortex*, 17(7), 1664–1671.

Hamilton, J., Chen, M., & Gotlib, I. 2013. Neural systems approaches to understanding major depressive disorder: An intrinsic functional organization perspective. *Neurobiology of Disease*, 52, 4–11.

Hamitlon, J., Etkin, A., Furman, D., Lemus, M., Johnson, R., & Gotlib, I. 2012. Functional neuroimaging of major depressive disorder: A meta-analysis and new integration of baseline activation and neural response data. *American Journal of Psychiatry*, 169, 693–703.

Hannula, D., Tranel, D., & Cohen, N. 2006. The long and the short of it: Relational memory impairments in amnesia, even at short lags. *The Journal Of Neuroscience*, 26(32), 8352–8359.

Harvey, P., Zaki, J., Lee, J., Ochsner, K., & Green, M. 2013. Neural substrates of empathic accuracy in people with schizophrenia. *Schizophrenia Bulletin*, 39(3), 617–628.

Hebb, D. 1949. *The Organisation of Behaviour*. New York: Wiley.

Hoekert, M., Kahn, R., Pijnenborg, M., & Aleman, A. 2007 Impaired recognition and expression of emotional prosody in schizophrenia: Review and meta-analysis. *Schizophrenia Research*, 96(1–3), 135–145.

Horan, W.P., Reise, S.P., Kern, R.S., Lee, J., Penn, D.L., & Green, M.F. 2015. Structure and correlates of self-reported empathy in schizophrenia. *Journal of Psychiatric Research*, 66, 60–66.

Jablensky, A. 2000. Epidemiology of schizophrenia: The global burden of disease and disability. *European Archives of Psychiatry and Clinical Neuroscience*, 250(6), 274–285.

Jackson, P.L., Meltzoff, A.N., & Decety, J. 2005. How do we perceive the pain of others? A window into the neural processes involved in empathy. *Neuroimage*, 24(3), 771–779.

Johnstone, L., & Dallos, R. 2006. *Formulation in Psychology and Psychotherapy: Making Sense of People's Problems*. First Edition. Routledge.

Johnstone, L., & Dallos, R. 2013. Introduction to formulation. In *Formulation in Psychology and Psychotherapy* (pp. 21–37). Routledge.

Kahn, I., Andrews-Hanna, J., Vincent, J., Snyder, A., & Buckner, R. 2008. Distinct cortical anatomy linked to subregions of the medial temporal lobe revealed by intrinsic functional connectivity. *Journal of Neurophysiology*, 100(1), 129–139.

Kaouane, N., Porte, Y., Vallee, M., Brayda-Bruno, L., Mons, N., Calandreau, L. et al. 2012. Glucocorticoids can induce PTSD-like memory impairments in mice. *Science*, 335, 1510–1513.

Kays, J.L., Hurley, R.A., & Taber, K.H. 2012. The dynamic brain: neuroplasticity and mental health. *The Journal of Neuropsychiatry and Clinical Neurosciences*, 24(2), 118–124.

Kerr, A.L., Cheng, S.Y., & Jones, T.A. 2011. Experience-dependent neural plasticity in the adult damaged brain. *Journal of Communication Disorders*, 44(5), 538–548.

Kindt, M. 2014. A behavioural neuroscience perspective on the aetiology and treatment of anxiety disorders. *Behaviour Research and Therapy*, 62, 24–36.

Klingberg, T., Forssberg, H., & Westerberg, H. 2002. Increased brain activity in frontal and parietal cortex underlies the development of visuospatial working memory capacity during childhood. *Journal of Cognitive Neuroscience*, 14(1), 1–10.

Kohler, C., Walker, J., Martin, E., Healey, K., & Moberg, P. 2010. Facial emotion perception in schizophrenia: A meta-analytic review. *Schizophrenia Bulletin*, 36(5), 1009–1019.

Krugers, H., Zhou, M., Joels, M., & Kindt, M. 2011. Regulation of excitatory synapses and fearful memories by stress hormones. *Frontiers in Behavioural Neuroscience*, 5, 1–11.

Landgren, H., & Curtis, M.A. 2011. Locating and labeling neural stem cells in the brain. *Journal of Cellular Physiology*, 226(1), 1–7.

Lashley, K. 1929. *Brain Mechanisms and Intelligence: A Quantitative Study of Injuries to the Brain*. Chicago: University of Chicago Press.

LeDoux, J.E. 1996. The Emotional Brain Simon Schuster. New York, 384.

Lee, J., Quintana, J., Nori, P., & Green, M. 2011. Theory of mind in schizophrenia: Exploring neural mechanisms of belief attribution. *Social Neuroscience*, 6(5-6), 569–581.

Lee, J., & Park, S. 2005. Working memory impairments in schizophrenia: A meta-analysis. *Journal of Abnormal Psychology*, 114(4), 599.

Leuner, B., & Gould, E. 2010. Structural plasticity and hippocampal function. *Annual Review of Psychology*, 61, 111–140.

Li, H., Chan, R., McAlonan, G., & Gong, Q. 2010. Facial emotion processing in schizophrenia: A meta-analysis of functional neuroimaging data. *Schizophrenia Bulletin*, 36(5), 1029–1039.

Lieberman, M.D. 2007. Social cognitive neuroscience: A review of core processes. *Annual Review of Psychology*, 58, 259–289.

McCabe, R., Bullenkamp, J., Hansson, L., Lauber, C., Martinez-Leal, R., Rössler, W. et al. 2012. The therapeutic relationship and adherence to antipsychotic medication in schizophrenia. *PLoS One*, 7(4), e36080.

McDougall, G.J. 1990. A review of screening instruments for assessing cognition and mental status in older adults. *The Nurse Practitioner*, 15(11), 18.

Montag, C., Dziobek, I., Richter, I., Neuhaus, K., Lehmann, A., Sylla, R., Heekeren, H., Heinz, A., & Gallinat, J. 2011. Different aspects of theory of mind in paranoid schizophrenia: Evidence from a video-based assessment. *Psychiatry Research*, 186(2-3), 203–209.

Moretti, M., Segal, Z., McCann, C., Shaw, B., Miller, D., & Vella, D. 1996 Self-referent versus other-referent information processing in dysphoric, clinically depressed, and remitted depressed subjects. *Personality and Social Psychology Bulletin*, 22, 68–80.

Moscovitch, M. 1995. Recovered consciousness: a hypothesis concerning modularity and episodic memory. *Journal of Clinical and Experimental Neuropsychology*, 17(2), 276–290.

Paris, J. 2013. Psychiatry and Neuroscience. *The Canadian Journal of Psychiatry*, 54(8), 513–517.

Passarotti, A. 2014. Neurocognitive models of evolving bipolar disorder in youth, in Stakowski, S., Del Bello, M., & Adler, C. (eds.) *Progression of Bipolar Disorder in Youth: Presentation, Treatment, and Neurobiology*. New York: Oxford University Press.

Pavuluri, M. 2014. Neurobiology of bipolar disorder in youth, in Strakowski, S., Adler, C., & Del Bello, M. (eds.) *Bipolar Disorder in Youth*. 1st edn. New York: Oxford University Press.

Pavuluri, M. 2015. Neuroscience-based formulation and treatment for early-onset bipolar disorder: A paradigm shift. *Current Treatment Options in Psychiatry*, 2, 229–251.

Pedersen, A., Koelkebeck, K., Brandt, M., Wee, M., Kueppers, K., Kugel, H., Kohl, W., Bauer, J., & Ohrmann, P. 2012. Theory of mind in patients with schizophrenia: Is mentalizing delayed? *Schizophrenia Research*, 137(1–3), 224–229.

Persons, J. 2008. *The Case Formulation Approach to Cognitive Behaviour Therapy*. London: Guildford.

Posner, J., Stewart, J., & Rieder, R. 2007. Neurobiological formulations: Integrating clinical and biological psychiatry. *Academic Psychiatry*, 31(6), 479–484.

Restifo, S. 2010. An empirical categorization of psychosocial factors for clinical case formulation and treatment planning. *Australasian Psychiatry*, 18(3), 210–213.

Sacher, J., Neumann, J., Funfstuck, T., Soliman, A., Villringer, A., & Schroeter, M. 2012. Mapping the depressed brain: A meta-analysis of structural and functional alterations in major depressive disorder. *Journal of Affective Disorders*, 140, 142–148.

Sala, R., Axelson, D., & Birmaher, B. 2009. Phenomenology, longitudinal course, and outcome of children and adolescents with pipolar spectrum disorders. *Child and Adolescent Psychiatry Clinics of North America*, 18(2), 273–289.

Seitz, A., & Watanabe, T. 2005. A unified model for perceptual learning. *Trends in Cognitive Sciences*, 9(7), 329–334.

Schoenfeld, T.J., & Gould, E. 2012. Stress, stress hormones, and adult neurogenesis. *Experimental neurology*, 233(1), pp.12–21.

Shapiro, Y. 2014. Psychodynamic formulation in the age of neuroscience: A dynamical systems model. *Psychoanalytic Dialogues*, 24(2), 175–192.

Singh, M., & Gotlib, I. 2014. The neuroscience of depression: Implications for assessment and intervention. *Behaviour Research and Therapy*, 62, 60–73.

Smith, M., Horan, W., Karpouzian, T., Abram, S., Cobia, D., & Csernansky, J. 2012. Self- reported empathy deficits are uniquely associated with poor functioning in schizophrenia. *Schizophrenia Research*, 137(1-3), 196–202.

Sprong, M., Schothorst, P., Vos, E., Hox, J., & van Engeland, H. 2007. Theory of mind in schizophrenia: Meta-analysis. *The British Journal of Psychiatry: The Journal of Mental Science*, 191, 5–13.

Squire, L.R., & Zola-Morgan, S. 1991. The medial temporal lobe memory system. *Science*, 253(5026), 1380–1386.

Steer, R., Beck, A., Clark, D., & Beck, J. 1994. Psychometric properties of the cognition checklist with psychiatric outpatients and university students. *Psychological Assessment*, 6, 67–70.

Sugranyes, G., Kyriakopoulos, M., Corrigall, R., Taylor, E., & Frangou, S. 2011. Autism spectrum disorders and schizophrenia: Meta-analysis of the neural correlates of social cognition. *PLOS ONE*, 6, 10.

Suzuki, M., Hagino, H., Nohara, S., Zhou, S., Kawasaki, Y., Takahashi, T., Matsui, M., Seto, H., Ono, T., & Kurachi, M. 2005. Male-specific volume expansion of the human hippocampus during adolescence. *Cerebral Cortex*, 15(2), 187–193.

Taylor, S., Kang, J., Brege, I., Tso, I., Hosanagar, A., & Johnson, T. 2012. Meta-analysis of functional neuroimaging studies of emotion perception and experience in schizophrenia. *Biological Psychiatry*, 71(2), 136–145.

Valenstein, E. 1998. *Blaming the Brain: The Truth about Drugs and Mental Health*. New York: Free Press.

Visser, R., Scholte, H., Beemsterboer, T., & Kindt, M. 2013. Neural pattern similarity predicts long-term fear memory. *Nature Neuroscience*, 16, 388–390.

West, A., Weinstein, S., Peters A., Katz, A., Henry D., Cruz, R. et al. 2014. Child and family-focused cognitive-behavioural therapy for pediatric bipolar disorder: A randomized clinical Trial. *Journal of the American Academy of Child and Adolescent Psychiatry*, 54(3), 1168–1178.

Whisman, M.A. 1993. Mediators and moderators of change in cognitive therapy of depression. *Psychological Bulletin*, 114(2), 248.

Wible C. G. (2012). Schizophrenia as a disorder of social communication. *Schizophrenia Research and Treatment*, 2012, Article ID 920485. doi:10.1155/2012/920485

Wible, C. 2013. Hippocampal physiology, structure and function and the neuroscience of schizophrenia: A unified account of declarative memory deficits, working memory deficits and schizophrenic symptoms. *Behavioral Sciences (Basel, Switzerland)*, 3(2), 298–315.

Wible, C., Shenton, M., & McCarley, R. 1997. Functional neuroanatomy of the limbic system and planum temporale, in Krishnan, R., & Doraiswamy, P. (eds.) *Brain Imaging in Clinical Psychiatry*. New York: Dekker, 63–101.

Wosiski-Kuhn, M., & Stranahan, A.M. 2012. Opposing effects of positive and negative stress on hippocampal plasticity over the lifespan. *Ageing research reviews*, 11(3), pp.399–403.

Yudofsky, S., & Hales, R. 2004. *Essentials of Neuropsychiatry and Behavioral Neurosciences*. Washington, DC: American Psychiatric Publishing.

Chapter 4

Diet and nutrition

Mary Kelly and Patrick Ryan

CHAPTER TOPICS

- Review of the literature on diet, nutrition and mental health
- The role of dietary information in psychological assessment and formulation
- Structured assessment tools to assess dietary behaviours and nutritional intake
- Sample open-ended questions relating to diet and nutrition to be considered for use in a clinical interview

Introduction

Clinical formulation has been defined in a variety of ways, but most would agree that it extends beyond a basic hypothesis of the client's difficulties, and represents the way in which we draw together theoretical knowledge and the lived experiences of our clients in a meaningful, collaborative way that helps both the client and therapist reach a clearer understanding about the struggles the client is facing (Adame 2015). Standard clinical interviews tend to gather a myriad of information, ranging from the specific presenting symptoms to the general impact of psychological malaise and distress. Some of this information may appear usable and relevant, whilst more is deemed peripheral to assessment, diagnosis or intervention. More often than not, if this information is difficult to fit into a preferred formulation model, it is excluded from the process (Johnstone and Dallos 2013). Consequently, information that may be pertinent to the treatment and intervention of the client's distress is inevitably lost.

This chapter encourages the practitioner to consider how information related to diet and nutrition gleaned directly and indirectly during clinical encounters can be used to assist with the formulation process. The literature on diet and nutrition in mental health is reviewed, highlighting the pertinent information that can be utilised throughout the consultation process. What we eat affects how we think and feel every day of our lives, thus should represent a fundamental component of a comprehensive approach to mental health care. Indeed, the links between diet, nutrition and psychological well-being are gathering support from academic and clinical research communities, with ample research developed through a psychological perspective that examines the influence that this factor has on psychological functioning (Psaltopoulou et al. 2013; Lai et al. 2014; Rahe et al. 2014; Sarris et al. 2015). This chapter encourages the practitioner to consider how information related to diet and nutrition gleaned during the clinical engagement process may be used to assist with psychological formulation, by complementing traditional models of constructing formulation. The task then, is to explore how this information may be effectively captured during the therapeutic dialogue. The validity of current measures available to practitioners needs to be established to see which are best suited to generating a comprehensive profile of the client in distress. Finally, a clear and coherent integration of this specific data with other clinical information is necessary to help understand and contextualise a client's distress, and to generate specific hypotheses that could be administered in a clinical interview to enhance the formulation process.

It is acknowledged that specific mental health problems such as anorexia nervosa and bulimia are associated specifically with issues around food and diet amongst others. This chapter does not refer to such difficulties, but rather focuses on the more implicit impact of dietary and nutritional information on mental health in general.

Diet, nutrition and mental health

Nutrition and mental health intersect in many ways. Just like the heart or the liver, the brain is a bodily organ that is acutely sensitive to intake of food and drink. To remain healthy, it requires varying amounts of complex carbohydrates, fatty acids, amino acids, minerals and vitamins. The brain functions every hour of every day and continues to function through periods of sleep. It therefore requires a constant supply of fuel to work effectively, and that 'fuel' essentially comes from the food that we eat. A substantial portion of the global burden of disease is purported to be attributable to mental health conditions (Whiteford et al. 2013) and nutrition is hypothesised to have a greater impact on disease risk than any other individual item (Sarris et al. 2015). Like an expensive car, the brain functions best when it's filled up with premium fuel, for example, a diet rich in high-quality foods, minerals, vitamins and antioxidants that nourish the brain. On the flip side however, just like an expensive car, the brain can be damaged if poor quality fuel is ingested, for example, processed and refined foods. While diet and nutrition are primarily influential in optimising the structure and function of neurons and brain centres, it is also important to mention their influence on the immune system, brain plasticity and antioxidant defence, which directly impact both physical and mental health (Molendijk et al., 2011; Berk et al., 2013; Logan and Jacka, 2014; Sarris et al., 2015).

The following section will offer a review of the literature on diet, nutrition and mental health to offer context prior to exploring the integration of this nutritional and dietary information into psychological formulation. Studies have ranged from examining individual responses to dietary changes in randomised controlled trials (RCTs), to population-based cross-cultural comparisons of mental health and food intake.

The ground-breaking but controversial Minnesota Starvation Experiment carried out by Keys and colleagues (1950), was one of the first projects to offer seminal insights into diet, nutrition and their link to psychology. The study aimed to examine the effects of long-term semi-starvation on people's health and found that the semi-starved participants presented with significant increases in depression, hysteria and hypochondriasis. Participants became preoccupied with food, both during the starvation period and the rehabilitation phase. Sexual interest and social interaction were significantly reduced. All participants experienced a decline in concentration, comprehension and judgment capabilities. Physically, the participants experienced a drop in basal metabolic rate, reflected in reduced body temperature, respiration and heart rate. This study was a fundamental research catalyst in emphasising the link between diet, nutrition and mental health and is frequently cited in research exploring eating disorders.

In more recent times, Lai and colleagues (2014) completed a meta-analysis of 21 studies which examined the link between diet, nutrition and depression. They compared a 'healthy' Mediterranean diet with an 'unhealthy' Western diet. In general, a Mediterranean diet is characterised by large intakes of plant foods including fruit, vegetables, breads, cereals, and olive oil with a moderate intake of dairy, fish and poultry and low intake of red meat. A Western 'unhealthy' diet is characterised by processed or fried foods, refined grains, sugary products, and beer. The findings indicated that Mediterranean diets were significantly correlated with a reduced risk of depression. Western diets high in processed foods did not have a significant relationship with depression. Other studies have examined the impact of such a Mediterranean diet on individual health, with a meta-analysis of 22 studies confirming that the incidence of stroke, depression and cognitive impairment were lower for people engaged in a Mediterranean diet (Psaltopoulou et al. 2013). Rahe et al. (2014) completed a systematic review of 16 observational research studies examining the relationship between dietary patterns (Mediterranean versus Western) and depression in healthy adults, reporting that the majority of studies indicated a healthy Mediterranean diet had significant correlation with positive mental health, whereas an unhealthy western diet was linked to depression. Finally, Nanri et al. (2013) analysed data of 40,752 men and 48,285 women who participated in a Japanese public health survey between 1995 and 1998. They found that a 'prudent' dietary pattern (again, reflecting a Mediterranean diet) including a high intake of vegetables, fruits, potatoes, soy products, mushrooms, seaweed and fish was significantly correlated to a decreased risk of suicide. Other dietary patterns (Westernised) were not significantly correlated with suicide risk in either direction.

Such findings appear consistent across gender, culture and age group. For example, O'Neil et al. (2014) performed a systematic review which found that there was a link between unhealthy diets and poorer mental health in children. Similar findings are evident in Western European societies. Jacka et al. (2010) completed a cohort study of 3,000 adolescents from East London, ranging in age from 11 to 14 years who were ethnically diverse and socially deprived. They found that adolescents identified as having low quality diets were twice as likely to present with symptoms of depression as compared with adolescents with healthier diets.

KEY POINT

Food influences our mood, regardless of gender, culture or age group.

Studies investigating the potential generative mechanisms between diet and mental health have proposed a number of plausible biological pathways, although such associations should be interpreted with caution, as much of the research is cross-sectional in nature. Foods representative of the healthy, Mediterranean diet contain anti-inflammatory properties which influence concentrations of monoamines (a type of neurotransmitter in the brain) which are believed to play a role in the regulation of emotion and cognition (Kiecolt-Glaser 2010). Fruit and vegetables are rich in anti-oxidant compounds, which may reduce oxidative stress-induced neuronal damage, particularly neurons in the hippocampus which forms an important part of the limbic system (the region that regulates emotions; Lethem & Orrell 1997; Calder et al. 2009). A common mechanism between depression and cardio-metabolic disorders (Sanchez-Villegas & Martinez-Gonzalez 2013) has drawn attention to the potential role of inflammatory processes in the diet-depression relationship, and recent evidence suggests that women with a diet of high pro-inflammatory potential were more likely to develop recurrent depression over the following five-year period (Akbaraly et al. 2016).

Assessment

The importance of collecting vital data on lifestyle factors throughout assessment is not a novel idea. It is widely accepted that key lifestyle factors can act as both causal and intervention opportunities for psychological distress, and that they can promote well-being and cognitive functioning when used effectively. Despite this, psychologists and healthcare professionals still often overlook the significance of lifestyle factors such as diet and nutrition throughout the consultation process, and a comprehensive approach to the understanding of basic, but core experiences rarely finds its way into standardised assessment or treatment. The following studies outline several clinical presentations in psychological services that may be directly or indirectly related to clients' diet and nutrition, reiterating the fundamental importance of gathering such information in the first instance.

- Halfon et al. (2013) conducted a cross-sectional analysis of 43,297 children on the 2007 American National Survey of Children's Health. Children who were categorised as obese were more likely to report poor health, grade repetition, school problems, attention deficit hyperactivity disorder (ADHD), conduct disorder, depression, learning disability and developmental delays.

- Ratcliffe and Ellison (2015) found that people with obesity often experience stigma and that this is internalised in negative self-evaluation which can result in psychological distress.
- Dipasquale et al. (2013) conducted a systematic review of 31 studies on schizophrenia and dietary patterns. They concluded that people with schizophrenia typically had a diet with high intake of saturated fat and low intake of fibre and fruit which leads to a higher rate of metabolic abnormalities and ultimately high risk of mortality from cardiovascular disease. The researchers had previously hypothesised that the reason for the high rates of metabolic disorder in schizophrenia was related to several factors including antipsychotic treatment, high levels of stress and unhealthy lifestyle, such as poor diet (Dipasquale et al. 2013).

Such research highlights that while the client's reason for presenting to mental health services may be due to traditional clinical issues such as conduct disorder, schizophrenia, depression or learning disability, it is essential that underlying factors such as diet and nutrition and their possible role and influence on the presenting condition are thoroughly explored.

KEY POINT

It is important to consider the potential influence of diet and nutrition on the client's reported difficulties, even when it is not the client's reason for presenting for help.

A key but often overlooked factor in determining the potential for a positive outcome to psychological intervention, is the readiness and capacity of the client to undertake the work – taking account of the client's current status of dietary and nutritional intake might be an important component in determining that capacity. Basic cognitive functioning such as attention and concentration requires a certain level of nutritional sustenance to support brain functioning (Logan and Jacka 2014). Indeed, the human brain has a high metabolic rate and uses the majority of calories consumed, for both structural and functional activities (Sarris et al. 2015), thus optimal brain function is greatly dependent on receiving sufficient and high quality amino acids, fats, vitamins and minerals (Berk et al. 2013; Logan and Jacka 2014). Higher-order, executive cognitive skills such as access to long term memory and abstract problem-solving demand even more from the nutritional value of food being consumed. With this in mind, before a formulation of any presenting problem is considered, a pre-formulation of client capacity to engage in demanding psychological work may be of benefit. If a particularly low body mass index (BMI) is suspected, the practitioner is advised to refer their client on for a physical screening before continuing with therapy, in line with best practice guidelines, as their client's cognition, emotion and physiology may be impaired due to malnutrition (Keys et al. 1950; NICE Guidelines 2017).

KEY POINT

Extremely poor diet and nutrition may impact the readiness and capacity of the client to undertake psychological work.

Integrating diet and nutrition into formal psychometric assessment

A comprehensive client profile is generated by employing the science of empirical assessment tools alongside the art of the clinical interview and creatively moulding this information into a formulation through the lens of a psychological model (Cates 1999). Many comprehensive measures of psychological distress reflect Carr and McNulty's (2016) model which proposes that assessment should begin with a broad intake measure, for example, a detailed clinical interview. If particular symptoms are identified (including symptoms related to diet and nutrition), then a more detailed standardised instrument should be administered. If scores on these measures are elevated, then a rigorous structured interview to assess psychological distress from a syndromal perspective is implemented. A plethora of assessment tools relating to diet and nutrition are available to the practitioner, a number of which have been summarised in the Table 4.1 below.

Table 4.1 Validated assessment tools to assess dietary behaviours and nutritional intake

Author (year)	Title	Application
Paxton et al. (2011)	Starting the Conversation (STC) – Diet	Simplified food frequency instrument to assess dietary behaviours
Hunot et al. (2016)	Adult Eating Behaviour Questionnaire (AEBQ)	Self-report measure of appetitive traits
Blake et al. (2013)	The Eating Identity Type Inventory (EITI)	Assesses affinity with four eating identity types; healthy, meat, picky and emotional.
Gleaves et al. (2013)	Eating Habits Questionnaire	Assesses cognitions, behaviours and feelings related to an extreme focus on healthy eating
Hemio et al. (2014)	Food Intake Questionnaire	Estimates daily nutrient intake and diet quality
Greenwood et al. (2012)	Healthy Eating Vital Sign (HEVS)	Assesses eating behaviours associated with excess weight

Such inventories can be utilised as formal assessments where appropriate, or alternatively may be useful to launch a dialogue between the client and therapist around certain dietary behaviours, that may ultimately contribute to a more useful clinical case formulation for the client.

KEY POINT

Inventories and questionnaires can be used in a more informal manner – working through them with the client may be a useful way of stimulating a necessary discussion around diet and nutrition.

Clinical interview questions on diet and nutrition

According to Carr and McNulty (2016) the most important factor in the initial clinical interview, is to use therapeutic questioning that refines and reviews preliminary formulations while constructing a positive therapeutic alliance and providing helpful feedback. This will facilitate the construction of a context of the psychological distress including the predisposing, precipitating, presenting, perpetuating, and protective factors. Palmer (2014) has advised that best practice when assessing diet and nutrition should focus on promoting the individual's autonomy and choice, alongside a careful and precise collection of the individual's narrative. Questions should facilitate an exploration of psychological, social and biological factors. Palmer (2014) suggests that when assessing eating behaviour, the clinical psychologist should address eating patterns and attitude towards weight, and ensure open questioning to allow for the possible exploration of unusual and hidden behaviours, which may not be revealed through direct questioning (Palmer 2014). The following emphatic, open-ended questions related to diet and nutrition should be considered for use in a clinical interview to enhance formulation.

- How would you describe your understanding of healthy eating behaviours?
- Describe a typical day of eating/meals for you
- What types of eating places do you frequently visit? Fast-food/restaurant?
- What kinds of food do you crave?
- When, if ever, do you eat during the night?
- What type of shopper are you – daily/weekly; planned/unplanned?
- How do you choose your food when you go food shopping?
- How important is a healthy diet to your overall lifestyle?
- What is your understanding of a healthy diet?
- What do your friends and family say about your eating?
- How would you describe your relationship with food?
- Have you embarked on diets/changes to your nutrition in the past? What has been your experience of these?

All common models of practice and theoretical orientation promote the use of detailed assessment interviews and reflective counselling skills in order to assist the client with self-awareness and consequently identify if external non-clinical variables are perpetuating the problem (Carr and McNulty 2016). Given the evidence base presented earlier in the chapter, the challenge to mental health professionals will be to use these more explicitly pertaining to diet and nutrition. Diet and nutrition may also account for some practitioner frustration during formulation, as its influence on mental health may be quite significant, but covert (Stead et al. 2011; Halfon et al. 2013). Failing to acknowledge or address its influence may lead to a bit-part approach to integrating important information or making potentially significant information redundant, when in fact it could offer additional or alternative ways of constructing intervention, objectives. Formulation must be generated through a powerful therapeutic dialogue that captures all relevant information from the client, in order to create a holistic mapping of the client's presentation (Johnstone and Dallos 2013), and not just about the parts that fit with pre-determined categories that may or may not apply to the specific client.

Initiating therapeutic dialogue and integrating models

From a psychological perspective, therapeutic dialogue is construed as the mechanism through which people make sense of their world and how they communicate this through language (Linnell, 2009). In-depth and skilled therapeutic dialogue is required to accurately identify relevant dietary and nutritional information as an influential variable in the client's presenting problem (Johnstone and Dallos 2013). The course of the therapeutic dialogue is often based on the psychological model being implemented. Take for example a client who is experiencing weight gain as a result of psychiatric treatment involving clozapine, olanzapine or quetiapine. Research suggests that this has a negative impact on compliance (Shrivastava and Johnston 2010). The skilled therapist will be aware of this scientific research and will tease out information on diet and nutrition during the therapeutic dialogue to ascertain its possible influence on attitudes towards medication, compliance and recovery. Various models will focus on different factors. Cognitive Behavioural Therapy (CBT) models may be very structured and orientated in the present and may focus on the issue of non-compliance and its current effect on psychological distress. Psychodynamic models may be more open-ended and past-orientated and may hone in on the individual's historical views of body shape, weight and feelings towards medication. Developmental models that examine change over time may look at the trajectory of compliance over the client's treatment history (Carr 2008).

The experienced therapist will be aware that all models ultimately have the same intention of exploring the client's psychological distress by collaboratively examining a range of variables to move towards improving their mental state (Rostworowska and Opoczyńska 2009; The British Psychological Society 2011). A comprehensive and integrative model will be the most appropriate in facilitating the fusion of information from the therapeutic dialogue to gain a clear and holistic map of the client's medication compliance, dietary patterns and related psychological distress. Effective methods of creating a therapeutic dialogue to acquire information on diet and nutrition can be drawn from leading researchers in eating disorder domains (Gilbert and Miles 2014; Palmer 2014), or existing best practice guidelines (e.g. NICE Guidelines 2017). Such sources indicate that the therapeutic dialogue must be open-ended but should allow for direct questioning on occasion to ascertain the specifics and individuality of each person. Finally, during the process of therapeutic dialogue, it is helpful to be cognisant that all people engage in two concurrent dialogues – one inner and one outer (Guregård and Seikkula 2013). Practitioners must be aware that regardless of the outer therapeutic dialogue and the psychological theory employed to create a formulation, that 'a map is never the actual territory' (Rostworowska and Opoczyńska 2009, p. 29). Best practice in formulation proposes that the formulation is based on integrated psychological research, it is collaboratively devised using appropriate language, it is a holistic, reflective and continuous process centred on personal meaning, and it is useful for the client (The British Psychological Society 2011). This collaborative, integrative and positive therapeutic alliance will foster a dialogue that can facilitate the identification of important clinical and non-clinical variables, such as diet and nutrition that will subsequently assist the formulation and intervention process.

Merging symptomatic and non-symptomatic information

Regardless of the theoretical framework, the experienced therapist will be able to identify if diet and nutrition are influential factors when identifying the client's psychological distress, and integrate this into developing a plan for intervention that can be continually revised. This merging of the clinical and non-clinical information to understand the client's distress is a skilled process (Cates 1999). The following two studies offer an example of the potential complexity of merging clinical and non-clinical factors into formulation. Stead et al. (2011) engaged in research consisting of 12 focus groups with young people aged 13–15 years in the North East of England. They found that there was a symbolic and social meaning associated with healthy eating which conflicted with vital developmental steps in adolescence such as self-image and belonging to a peer group. They concluded that it was an emotional risk factor for teenagers to be viewed as healthy eaters. In total contrast, Gilbert and Meyer (2005) found that in a study of 143 female students, high fears of negative evaluation were linked to restrictive eating as participants hypothesised that low body weight would raise their peer status. Participants with high fears of negative evaluation also presented with low self-esteem, depression and body dissatisfaction. These studies draw attention to the complexity of diet and nutrition as relevant non-clinical factors, as well as the individuality of each client. Expert and skilled application of traditional psychological models including developmental and social models, is essential in merging diet and nutrition into formulation to gain a comprehensive perspective of the client and their presenting psychological distress.

Conclusion

As healthcare culture becomes more influenced by managerialism principles and increasingly focused on scientific evidence, the emerging trend to quantify, standardise and manualise psychological assessment and intervention has often resulted in mental health professionals following strict protocols which occasionally 'conflict with the individuality of human behaviour' (Shapiro 2002). This chapter has highlighted that diet and nutrition is a key contributor to both physical and mental health, and can play a part in routine assessment protocols. The process of formulation should be all-encompassing and incorporate, where possible, all relevant variables of influence across individual, interpersonal, biological, social and cultural domains. While empirical evidence has indicated that more educated and experienced clinicians are better attuned to notice secondary information that may facilitate the map-making process of formulation (Kendjelic and Eells 2007; Charman 2008; Kuyken et al. 2009; Eells et al. 2011; Girón et al. 2014), further efforts must be made to thoroughly integrate information on diet and nutrition into the therapeutic dialogue and clinical interviews, across all mental health practitioners. This will ensure that a comprehensive and contextualised profile of the client and their psychological distress can be obtained, and that pertinent information that may be relevant to assessment and intervention will not be neglected.

Reflective exercise

Working with a partner, assign someone to the role of the practitioner and someone to the role of John (27-year-old male presenting with low mood and insomnia) and conduct an intake interview. Include some of the questions outlined earlier to elicit information about John's dietary intake.

- In Round 1, John will divulge his daily routine that revolves primarily around his career in engineering and his involvement in the local rowing club. John follows a strict and wholesome routine for his meals, ensuring he is obtaining sufficient nutrients, proteins and carbohydrates to retain strength and power capabilities for the upcoming training season. He rarely varies from this pattern and if he does, he experiences intense anxiety that does not dissipate until he has re-established his routine.
- In Round 2, John will divulge his daily routine that revolves primarily around his career in engineering and his involvement in the local rowing club. John tends to skip meals, often grabbing an 'on the go' bar for breakfast as he runs out the door to work and not eating again until the fast food drive-thru on his route home from work.

In pairs, discuss two separate formulations that could arise out of these intake interviews. What are the similarities and differences between them? Consider the potential impact this might have on subsequent intervention planning.

REFERENCES

Adame, A.L. 2015 *Constructing a Thoughtful Formulation*. Philadelphia: Routledge.

Akbaraly, T.N., Kerleau, C., Myart, M., Chevallier, N., Ndiaye, L., Shivappa, N., Hebert, J.R., & Kivimaki, M. 2016 Dietary inflammatory index and recurrence of depressive symptoms: Results from the Whitehall II Study. *Clinical Psychological Science*, 4(6), 1125–1134.

Berk, M., Williams, L.J., Jacka, F.N. et al. 2013 So depression is an inflammatory disease, but where does the inflammation come from? *British Medical Council Med*, 1, 200.

Blake, C.E., Bell, B.A., Freedman, D.A., Colabianchi, N., & Liese, A.D. 2013 The Eating Identity Type Inventory (EITI). Development and associations with diet. *Appetite, 69*, 15–22.

Calder P.C., Albers R., Antoine J.-M. et al. 2009 Inflammatory disease processes and interactions with nutrition. *British Journal of Nutrition*, 101(suppl 1), 1–45.

Carr, A. 2008 Depression in young people: Description, assessment, and evidence-based treatment. *Developmental Neurorehabilitation*, 11(1), 3–15.

Carr, A., & McNulty, M. 2016 *The Handbook of Adult Clinical Psychology: An Evidence-Based Practice Approach*, 2nd edn. London: Routledge.

Cates, J.A. 1999 The art of assessment in psychology: Ethics, expertise, and validity. *Journal of Clinical Psychology*, 55(5), 631–641.

Charman, D.P. 2008 *Core Processes in Brief Psychodynamic Psychotherapy: Advancing Effective*. Routledge: New Jersey.

Dipasquale, S., Pariante, C.M., Dazzan, P., Aguglia, E., McGuire, P., & Mondelli, V. 2013 The dietary pattern of patients with schizophrenia: A systematic review. *Journal of Psychiatric Research*, 47(2), 197–207.

Eells T.D., Lombart K.G., Salsman, N., Kendjelic, E.M., Schneiderman, C.T., & Lucas, C.P. 2011 Expert reasoning in psychotherapy case formulation. *Psychotherapy Research*, 21(4), 385–399.

Gilbert, N., & Meyer, C. 2005 Fear of negative evaluation and the development of eating psychopathology: A longitudinal study among nonclinical women. *International Journal of Eating Disorders*, 37, 307–312.

Gilbert, P., & Miles, J. (Eds) 2014 *Body Shame: Conceptualisation, Research and Treatment*. London: Routledge.

Girón, M., Manjón-Arce, P., Puerto-Barber, J., Sánchez-García, E., & Gómez-Beneyto, M. 2014 Clinical interview skills and identification of emotional disorders in primary care. *American Journal of Psychiatry*, 155(4), 530–535.

Gleaves, D.H., Graham, E.C., & Ambwani, S. 2013 Measuring "Orthorexia". Development of the eating habits questionnaire. *The International Journal of Educational and Psychological Assessment*, 12(2), 1–18.

Greenwood, J.L.J., Lin, J., Arguello, D., Ball, T., & Shaw, J.M. 2012 Healthy eating vital sign: A new assessment tool for eating behaviours. *International Scholarly Research Network*, 2012, Article ID 734682.

Guregård, S., & Seikkula, J. 2013 Establishing therapeutic dialogue with refugee families. *Contemporary Family Therapy*, 36(1), 41–57.

Halfon, N., Larson, K., & Slusser, W. 2013 Associations between obesity and comorbid mental health, developmental, and physical health conditions in a nationally representative sample of US children aged 10 to 17. *Academic Paediatrics*, 13(1), 6–13.

Hemio, K., Polonen, A., Ahonen, K., Kosola, M., Viitasalo, K., & Lindstrom, J. 2014 A simple tool for diet evaluation in primary health care: Validation of a 16-item food intake questionnaire. *International Journal of Environmental Research and Public Health*, 11(3), 2683–2697.

Hunot, C., Fildes, A., Croker, H., Llewellyn, C.H., Wardle, J., & Beeken, R.J. 2016 Appetitive traits and relationships with BMI in adults: Development of the adult eating behaviour questionnaire. *Appetite*, 105, 356–363.

Jacka, F.N., Pasco, J.A., Mykletun, A., Williams, L.J., Hodge A.M., O'Reilly, S.L., Nicholson, G.C., Kotowicz, M.A., & Berk, M. 2010 Association of Western and traditional diets with depression and anxiety in women. *American Journal of Psychiatry*, 167(3), 305–311.

Johnstone, L., & Dallos, R. 2013 *Formulation in Psychology and Psychotherapy: Making Sense of People's Problems*. London: Routledge.

Kendjelic E.M., & Eells T.D. 2007 Generic psychotherapy case formulation training improves formulation quality. *Psychotherapy*, 44(1), 66–77.

Keys, A., Brožek, J., Henschel, A., Mickelsen, O., & Taylor, H.L. 1950 *The Biology of Human Starvation*. Minnesota: University of Minnesota Press.

Kiecolt-Glaser, J.K. 2010 Stress, food, and inflammation: psychoneuroimmunology and nutrition at the cutting edge. *Psychosomatic Medicine*, 72(365), 9.

Kuyken, W., Padesky C.A., & Dudley, R. 2009 *Collaborative Case Conceptualization: Working Effectively with Clients in Cognitive-Behavioral Therapy*. New York: Guilford Publications.

Lai, J.S., Hiles, S., Bisquera, A., Hure, A.J., McEvoy, M., & Attia, J. 2014 A systematic review and meta-analysis of dietary patterns and depression in community-dwelling adults. *American Journal of Clinical Nutrition*, 99(12), 181–197.

Lethem, R., & Orrell, M. 1997 Antioxidants and dementia. *Lancet*, 349, 1189–1190.

Linnell, P. 2009 *Rethinking Language, Mind, and World Dialogically*. Charlotte NC: Information Age Publishing.

Logan, A.C., & Jacka, F.N. 2014 Nutritional psychiatry research: an emerging discipline and its intersection with global urbanization, environmental challenges and the evolutionary mismatch. *Journal of Physiological Anthropology*, 33, 22.

Molendijk, M.L., Bus, B.A, Spinhoven, P, Penninx, B.W., Kenis, G., Prickaerts, J., Voshaar R.C., & Elzinga, B.M. 2011 Serum levels of brain-derived neurotrophic factor in major depressive disorder: state-trait issues, clinical features and pharmacological treatment. *Molecular Psychiatry*, 16(11), 1088–1095.

Nanri, A., Mizoue, T., Poudel-Tandukar, K., Noda, M., Kato, M., Kurotani, K., Goto, A., Oba, S., Inoue, M., & Tsugane, S. 2013 The Japan Public Health Center-based prospective study group; Dietary patterns and suicide in Japanese adults: The Japan Public Health Center-based prospective study. *The British Journal of Psychiatry*, 203(6), 422–427.

NICE Guidelines 2017 Eating Disorders: Recognition and Treatment [online], available: https://www.nice.org.uk/guidance/ng69 (accessed 05 April 2018).

O'Neil, A., Quirk, S.E., Housden, S., Brennan, S.L., Williams, L.J., Pasco, J.A., Berk, M., & Jacka, F.N. 2014 Relationship between diet and mental health in children and adolescents: A systematic review. *American Journal of Public Health*, 104, 31–42.

Palmer, B. 2014 *Helping People with Eating Disorders: A Clinical Guide to Assessment and Treatment.* London: John Wiley and Sons.

Paxton, A.E., Strycker, L.A., Toobert, D.J., Ammerman, A.S., & Glasgow, R.E. 2011 Starting the conversation performance of a brief dietary assessment and intervention tool for health professionals. *American Journal of Preventative Medicine*, 40(1), 67–72.

Psaltopoulou, T., Sergentanis, T.N., Panagiotakos, D.B., Sergentanis, I.N., Kosti, R., & Scarmeas, N. 2013 Mediterranean diet, stroke, cognitive impairment, and depression: A meta-analysis. *Annual Neurological*, 74(13), 580–591.

Rahe, C., Unrath, M., & Berger, K. 2014 Dietary patterns and the risk of depression in adults: A systematic review of observational studies. *European Journal of Nutrition*, 53(4), 997–1013.

Ratcliffe, D., & Ellison, N. 2015 Obesity and internalized weight stigma: A formulation model for an emerging psychological problem. *Behavioural and Cognitive Psychotherapy*, 43(02), 239–252.

Rostworowska, M., & Opoczyńska, M. 2009 From monologue towards therapeutic dialogue'. Some remarks about systemic family consultations in a psychiatric in-patient ward. *Archives of Psychiatry and Psychotherapy*, 2, 29–34.

Sanchez-Villegas, A., & Martinez-Gonzalez, M.A. 2013 Diet, a new target to prevent depression? *BMC Medicine,* 11, 3.

Sarris, J., Logan, A.C., Akbaraly, T.N., Amminger, P.A., Balanzá-Martínez, V., Freeman, M.P., & Hibbel, J. 2015 Nutritional medicine as mainstream in psychiatry. *The Lancet Psychiatry*, 2(3), 271–274.

Shapiro, D.S. 2002 Renewing the scientist-practitioner model. *Psychologist*, 15(5), 232.

Shrivastava, A., & Johnston, M.E. 2010 Weight-gain in psychiatric treatment: Risks, implications, and strategies for prevention and management. *Mens Sana Monographs*, 8(1), 53–68. http://doi.org/10.4103/0973-1229.58819

Stead, M., McDermott, L., MacKintosh, A.M., & Adamson, A. 2011 Why healthy eating is bad for young people's health: Identity, belonging and food. *Social Science and Medicine*, 72(7), 1131–1139.

The British Psychological Society 2011 Division of Clinical Psychology: Good Practice Guidelines on the Use of Psychological Formulation. Available online: https://www1.bps.org.uk/system/files/Public%20files/DCP/cat-842.pdf

Whiteford, H.A., Degenhardt, L., Rehm, J. et al. 2013 Global burden of disease attributable to mental and substance use disorders: Findings from the Global Burden of Disease Study 2010. *Lancet*, 383, 1575–1586.

Chapter 5

Personality

Patrick Ryan and Eve Pender

CHAPTER TOPICS

- Biological and environmental approaches to personality development
- Contribution of personality factors to psychological distress
- Formal and informal approaches to assessing personality
- The use of transference and countertransference in eliciting personality-related information

Introduction

Put succinctly, personality refers to the way in which a person consistently thinks, feels and behaves in various life domains. Over the decades, a wealth of academic research has documented the influence of personality factors on important life outcomes such as health, happiness and satisfaction, and as such, personality assessment tends to be a well-established component of the client's initial intake interview. In light of this, information on the client's personality may more readily integrated into the formulation process than information pertinent to domains of the client's sexuality or spirituality, for example. Nonetheless, the relevance of personality to this discussion of *formulation* must not be overlooked. As will be explored, integrating personality into a formulation ensures that a thoroughly holistic perspective of the client and their difficulties is captured, enhancing the validity and utility of the psychological formulation and strengthening the therapeutic relationship.

Regarded as the psychological equivalent of the body's immune system, personality influences the frequency of exposure to stressors as well as the individual's ability to cope with stressors. Biologically speaking, in everyday life each person is surrounded by contagious bacteria and the strength of an individual's defence system determines whether this bacteria infiltrates the body and leads to disease. When an individual's personality consists of numerous adaptive traits and relatively few maladaptive traits, the capacity to cope with stressors is strengthened. On the other hand, when personality comprises mainly maladaptive traits, the interaction of personality characteristics and even minor social stressors can lead to the development of psychological distress and difficulties (Millon et al. 2012). Personality explains from a biological, psychological and social perspective how a person relates to themselves, to others and to the world around them. Integrating this kind of information into a formulation ensures that it is meaningful and contextualised for each individual client, which is at the core of psychological formulation, setting it apart from other disciplines.

This chapter seeks to explore the complexity of personality development by discussing the personality theories that have been offered to date. These typically fall under the *biological* approach to personality development (i.e. temperament, trait theory) or the *environmental* approach to personality development (i.e. culture, characteristic adaptations, narrative identities). Following this, the empirical evidence that points to facets of personality as generative mechanisms in the development of psychological disorder and a client's experience of psychological distress will be discussed. This may offer some assistance to the reader in identifying aspects of personality that serve as protective, predisposing or maintaining factors in the context of their client's distress. The chapter will address personality assessment, which can take the form of standardised measures (such as the Millon Clinical Multiaxial Inventory or the NEO Personality Inventory) or more informal questioning, obtained throughout the clinical interview and beyond. Finally, the chapter encourages the reader to consider the relationship between the client's personality and their distress as an ongoing dynamic process, which unfolds through therapeutic dialogue, implicating important processes such as transference and countertransference.

Personality development

The importance of incorporating personality factors into the formulation process cannot be truly understood without first considering the manner in which an individual's personality develops. The development of personality represents a complex interplay of biological, environmental and psychological factors. Existing theories attempt to provide an explanation as to why some people generally experience psychological well-being and have the capacity to manage the stressors of daily life, while others experience frequent psychological distress and display maladaptive patterns of coping. Much of the research on personality development in recent decades has stipulated that inherited predispositions and physiological processes can be used to explain differences in personality. Within this, psychologists in the field have primarily examined temperament (inborn, genetically based differences in personality) and the presence or absence of certain traits (trait theories).

Temperament

Temperament relates to the biological potential for behaviour that manifests in the dominant mood of individuals and the intensity of their activity levels (Friedman et al. 2010). In practice, temperament describes a child's innate tendencies and behavioural style, which consists of self-regulation capacity and emotional reactivity (Kim and Kochanska 2012). Indeed, its appearance in early childhood has contributed largely to the belief that temperament is genetically based, with researchers identifying three different temperamental types in babies including 'difficult', 'easy' and 'slow to warm up' (Thomas and Chess 1977). Difficult temperament is indicative of later adjustment difficulties, including internalising and externalising difficulties, mood disorders and attention difficulties (Kim and Kochanska 2012). Longitudinal studies assessing the link between temperament and adult personality traits are relatively scarce, however some findings have suggested that children identified by their parents as 'inhibited' had a higher probability in adulthood to be rated as highly inhibited and experience internalising difficulties (Asendorpf, Denissen and Marcel 2008).

It has been argued that basic temperamental dimensions are simplistic versions of adult traits which develop gradually over time into adult personality through a genetically controlled process (Bender et al. 2014). Although temperament has an important influence on personality, it does not determine an individual's personality. Temperament constrains development through interaction with the individual's environment, directing it towards a certain pathway (Friedman et al. 2010). For example, a temperamentally approachable and smiley child will typically elicit warm and friendly responses from others which over time become the environments that help to reinforce and magnify these initial temperamental tendencies. The approachable, smiley child is likely to exhibit high extraversion in adulthood (Bender et al. 2014). The capacity of an infant to emotionally regulate is based on an interaction between temperamental characteristics and environmental influences (Calkins 2010). In this vein, whether a particular temperament develops into psychological difficulties or not is highly influenced by the caregiver's response to the child's temperament. Temperamentally difficult children are more sensitive to their environment, specifically parenting quality and attachment relationships (Calkins 2010). Parents who adjust their parenting style to accommodate for their child's temperament can reduce the biological vulnerability, whereas parents who respond negatively to the child's temperament may render a person vulnerable to developing psychological difficulties (Millon et al. 2012). Temperament may serve as either a protective factor or predisposing factor and as such, is an important aspect of an individual's personality to consider when formulating.

Trait theory

Trait theory is arguably the most prominent personality theory that has stemmed from the biological model. According to trait theory, dispositional traits which arise from temperament account for an individual's personality. Over the years, models with up to sixteen factors (Cattell 1957) and as few as two factors (Eysenck and Eysenck, 1963) have been proposed, with criticisms of being too broad and too narrow, respectively. The most widely accepted trait theory of personality is the Big Five model (also known as the Five Factor Model, McCrae and Costa 2008) (Figure 5.1) which somewhat hits the middle ground, and proposes that individual differences in personality can be accounted for by five traits; extraversion, neuroticism, agreeableness, conscientiousness and openness to experience. Each of these traits comprises more specific characters known as facets. For example, extraversion contains facets of warmth, gregariousness, assertiveness, activity, excitement seeking and positive emotionality. Regardless of the trait model one ascribes to, most psychologists agree that traits are the cornerstone of psychological individuality. Traits such as extraversion and agreeableness describe the most fundamental differences between people that are evident in people's behaviour, which is pervasive across situations and over time (Bender et al. 2014).

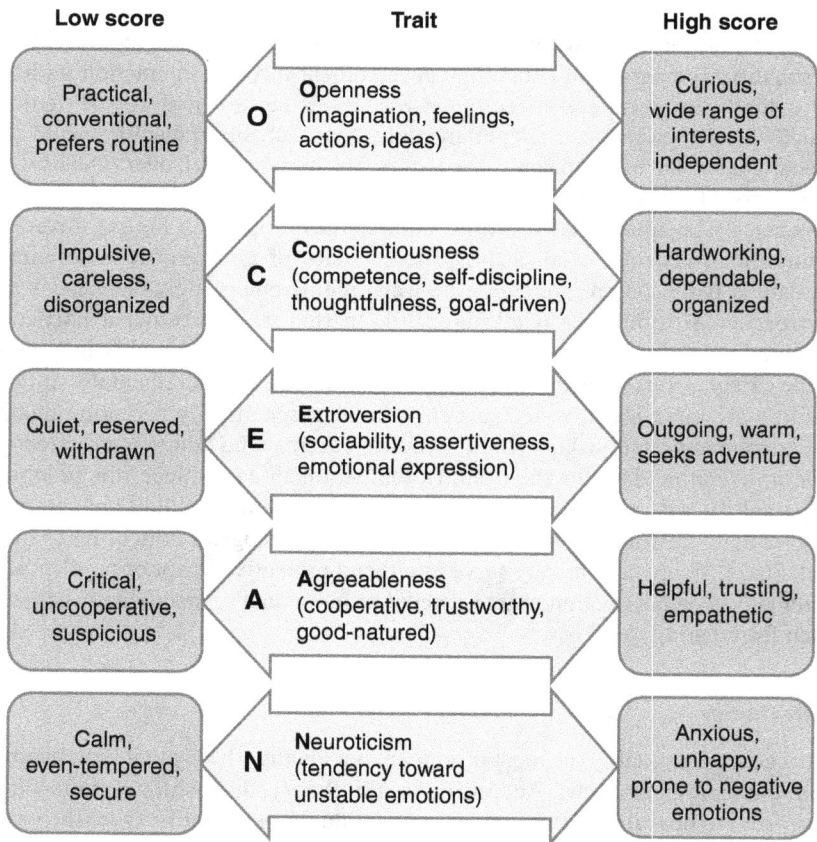

Low score	Trait	High score
Practical, conventional, prefers routine	**O**penness (imagination, feelings, actions, ideas)	Curious, wide range of interests, independent
Impulsive, careless, disorganized	**C**onscientiousness (competence, self-discipline, thoughtfulness, goal-driven)	Hardworking, dependable, organized
Quiet, reserved, withdrawn	**E**xtroversion (sociability, assertiveness, emotional expression)	Outgoing, warm, seeks adventure
Critical, uncooperative, suspicious	**A**greeableness (cooperative, trustworthy, good-natured)	Helpful, trusting, empathetic
Calm, even-tempered, secure	**N**euroticism (tendency toward unstable emotions)	Anxious, unhappy, prone to negative emotions

Figure 5.1 The Big Five personality traits (OCEAN).

KEY POINT

Personality traits are generally stable and pervasive across situations and over time.

Despite the majority of research on personality development focusing on temperament in early life and trait theories, the influence of environmental factors must not be overlooked. An individual's concept of self, their goals and their values do not develop within a vacuum, but rather develop in a complex, social world (McWilliams 2011). Factors such as culture (individualist versus collectivist), the tightness and complexity of social norms, child-rearing practices and parenting styles (permissive and easy-going versus restrictive and over-protective) all bear a substantial influence on the traits developed throughout the trajectory of childhood and adolescence (Anaya and Perez-Edgar 2018). As primary agents in the child's social and emotional development, parents choose what activities and games their child engages in, what playmates are invited over, what school they go to, which have implications for the development of personality (Reitz, Zimmermann, Hutteman, Specht and Neyer 2014; Syed and Seiffge-Krenke 2013).

Researchers have extended biologically based theories such as temperament and traits, to integrate concepts such as characteristic adaptations and narrative identity as constructs of personality. Initially, traits develop first as broad individual differences in temperament displayed by infants. Characteristic adaptations (which comprise a child's goals and motives and are highly influenced by the social environment; McWilliams 2011) result from the dynamic interaction between early personality traits and experience. As traits and characteristic adaptations continue to develop into adolescence and young adulthood, an individual constructs their narrative identity, viewed as an internalised and evolving story of the self which aims to provide a person's life with purpose, meaning and unity. These dispositional traits, characteristic adaptations and narrative identity relate to each other in a complex and meaningful manner which combine to construct the whole person (McAdams and Olson 2010).

Personality and psychological distress

Personality provides an explanation as to why some people can remain relatively intact following severely traumatic experiences, whilst others crumble under minor life stresses. Merging personality with other clinical information when developing a formulation enables the identification of facets of the client's personality that may serve as either protective, predisposing or maintaining factors. As the primary goal of formulation is to summarise and understand how a client's problems developed, focusing on the characteristic way in which the client thinks, feels, behaves and relates to themselves and others provides some very valuable information in this regard. Multiple mechanisms have been postulated to explain how personality impacts health and health-related behaviours. Indeed, personality factors are an important feature in the development of a number of psychological difficulties including eating disorders, substance abuse and PTSD.

The association between personality and psychopathology can be divided into three main relationships: Patho-plastic, spectrum and causal relationships. The patho-plastic relationship refers to the phenomenon that personality and psychopathology can influence the presentation of one another. A person's expression of psychopathology is influenced by their personality traits, similarly an individual's personality can be affected by the appearance of psychopathology (Widiger 2011). Spectrum relationships refer to the fact that personality and psychopathology may share a common aetiology. Causal relationships refer to the causal role that psychopathology and personality can have on the development of one another (Widiger 2011). Such associations are important to bear in mind while considering the research in this area. An overview of research that explores the relationship between personality and psychological well-being or distress is offered below.

KEY POINT

Personality and psychopathology have a complex, bi-directional relationship and can influence the presentation of one another.

Neuroticism

Empirical evidence indicates that the trait neuroticism is associated with a number of physical and psychological disorders (Lahey 2009; Widiger 2011; Coleman and Trunzo 2015), and has been found to negatively impact general well-being, happiness and overall life, job and marital satisfaction. People high in neuroticism have a tendency to worry, are highly reactive to stressful situations and are susceptible to distress even in the absence of stressful events (Widiger 2011). There are two primary ways by which neuroticism may have an impact on life outcomes: Reactive person-environment interactions and evocative person-environment interactions. In the former, people high in neuroticism react to events with high levels of distress, worry and anxiety, increasing their risk of experiencing psychological distress and developing a psychological disorder. In the latter, the negative reactions of others and poor decision making produced by a person's frequent expression of distress reinforces and magnifies the original stressor. Watson and Casillas (2003) postulated that neuroticism could be viewed as a strength as well as a weakness. Neuroticism may have adaptive features in that it enhances an individual's safety through hypervigilance and responsiveness to danger (Watson and Casillas 2003). Research examining this hypothesis has indicated that there is a curvilinear correlation between neuroticism and marital satisfaction, in which neuroticism may increase awareness and motivation to react proactively to marital difficulties (Daspe et al. 2013; Daspe et al. 2015).

KEY POINT

Personality traits can be both adaptive and maladaptive, depending on the individual context.

Substance abuse

Personality traits such as impulsivity have been implicated in the development of substance dependence and abuse. Coleman and Trunzo (2015) examined drug use, personality factors and stress among college students. The findings indicated that individuals who display neurotic personality traits and experience frequent stress are more susceptible to abusing substances. These findings should be interpreted with caution as the design was correlational and therefore causality cannot be inferred. Moreover, a number of other risk factors for substance abuse were not considered such as trauma, psychopathology, social support and biological factors.

Post-traumatic stress disorder (PTSD)

Personality features have been identified as risk and resiliency factors in the development of PTSD. The three factor personality model (externalizing, internalizing and simple) has been proposed to account for the heterogeneity in PTSD symptoms (Carleton et al. 2015). High social inhibition has been associated with increased avoidance whilst high negative affectivity has been associated with increased avoidance and arousal but fewer intrusive symptoms (Mommersteeg et al. 2011). Additionally, Castillo et al.'s (2014) study of soldiers suggested that the three personality profile subtypes distinguish PTSD from complex PTSD. Carleton et al.'s (2015) study investigated the PTSD personality-subtype model in a sample of 129 women exposed to domestic violence. Whilst only using self-report measures, the findings indicated that the internalising and externalising subtype groups presented with more complicated PTSD expressions with higher levels of comorbid symptomology such as depression and substance abuse.

Eating disorders

The onset of eating disorders provides a clear example of the importance of considering personality in a formulation. A high level of conscientiousness is associated with anorexia nervosa. A person with high levels of conscientiousness typically possesses self-discipline and achievement striving characteristics, which are vital attributes needed to succeed in extreme weight loss. In contrast, impulsiveness that is characteristic of bulimia and binge eating is associated with low scores in conscientiousness. Previous research indicates that people experiencing anorexia nervosa display perfectionistic and compulsive personality traits, whilst people diagnosed with bulimia display impulsivity (Cassin and von

Ranson 2005; Widiger 2011). In relation to eating disorders, a person's level of conscientiousness and impulsiveness could be viewed as a predisposing factor rendering the individual vulnerable to developing an eating difficulty.

Personality disorders

Personality disorders can be debilitating and negatively impact interpersonal relationships and occupational functioning (Carver and Connor-Smith 2010; Hasin et al. 2011; Blasco-Fontecilla et al. 2014). It is widely accepted that personality disorders are maladaptive variations of general personality traits. For example, Obsessive Compulsive Personality Disorder can be understood as an extreme maladaptive variation of conscientiousness (Hasin et al. 2011).

Personality disorders are characterised by maladaptive pathological features (Millon et al. 2012). People with personality disorders exhibit a lack of resilience at times of stress and are adaptively inflexible. An individual with a personality disorder attempts to control interpersonal situations through the intensity and rigidity of their traits. As the person cannot be flexible, the environment needs to adjust to the person. When the environment cannot be adjusted, a crisis arises. The inflexibility and frequent crises reduce the opportunity for the person to acquire new adaptive strategies (Millon et al. 2012).

It has been proposed that personality disorders should be viewed as chronic and pervasive variants of mental health disorders rather than distinct entities. Reflective of this, are proposals for the DSM-5 to abandon the classification of personality disorders and merge personality disorders with other psychiatric disorders. For example, avoidant personality disorder could be converted into generalized social phobia, obsessive compulsive disorder could be converted into a severe form of OCD, borderline personality disorder (BPD) into a mood disorder and schizotypal personality disorder into schizophrenia (Hasin et al. 2011). The ICD-10 already classifies schizotypal personality disorder as a variant of schizophrenia. As some individuals have personality disorders that are not currently adequately described by one or even multiple personality disorders, it is plausible that they would not be better defined by an assortment of anxiety, mood or psychotic diagnoses (Skodol, Bender and Morey 2014).

Previous studies have indicated that personality disorders are correlated with suicidal ideation and intent (Wedig et al. 2012; Blasco-Fontecilla et al. 2014; Ansell et al. 2015). For example, Narcissistic Personality Disorder is associated with more lethal attempts of suicide (Miller et al. 2013; Blasco-Fontecilla et al. 2014). Research indicates that BPD severity uniquely predicts frequency of suicide attempts over other personality disorders (Wedig et al. 2012; Ansell et al. 2015). The documented association between personality disorders and suicide provides further evidence for the importance of integrating personality factors into a psychological formulation.

The aforementioned empirical evidence lends support to the premise that personality is an important factor to consider when evaluating how a person experiences psychological distress. Adding personality influences to a formulation extends the understanding of the client's difficulties and enhances the psychological formulation by indicating where intervention may or may not be effective. For example, targeting a relatively stable trait for substantial change may be less effective than learning how to manage that trait when it is likely to be problematic. Providing feedback to clients on a psychological formulation which incorporates their personality traits will broaden the understanding of the client's strengths and difficulties and will help determine if more innate factors for example temperament, may be more or less open to psychological intervention.

It is important to note that the relationship between personality and psychopathology is not unidirectional, but rather bi-directional. A person's characteristic way of feeling, thinking, behaving and relating to others can either contribute to or result in the development of psychological distress and even psychopathology (Widiger 2011). In a similar manner, pervasive and severe psychological distress can have a lasting effect on a person's characteristic manner of thinking, feeling and behaving, leading to fundamental personality changes including the development of new personality traits. The ICD-10 recognises the impact of psychopathology on personality and includes a diagnosis for personality change ancillary to a traumatic experience and/ or psychiatric disorder (Shedler et al. 2014).

Personality assessment

A comprehensive assessment comprising a clinical intake interview and standardised measures can be necessary to develop a complete formulation of the client's difficulties (Carr and McNulty 2006). A personality assessment serves to provide a substantive and integrative understanding of the client across varying life areas (Hopwood et al. 2008), thus providing a comprehensive profile of the client in distress. Such information can be obtained informally or formally, as discussed below.

Informal personality assessment

Self-report personality questionnaires as examined later in the chapter can provide a personality profile which may highlight the interplay between current presenting difficulties and enduring personality patterns (Millon et al. 2012). However, self-report measures should not be used in isolation to assess an individual's personality. Rather, the personality profile should be combined with information obtained through the clinical interview and if appropriate, collateral information from other team members and family members. A number of questions could be included in the initial interview to assess an individual's personality including:

- Describe your early life experiences.
- How do you cope with stressful situations?
- How do you describe yourself?

- What do you value in life?
- How would others describe you?
- Describe your current/previous relationships?
- Describe your current goals/motivations?
- How do you typically think about and cope with challenges you face?

The assessment of an individual's personality and the relationship between their personality, their environment and symptomology should not be solely completed during the initial assessment. It is an on-going, cumulative and iterative process across all encounters as the knowledge obtained about client's ways of thinking, feeling and behaving in various situations unfolds over time as the therapeutic relationship develops.

Standardised measures

Personality traits are typically measured by using self-report questionnaires. The use of self-report measures is advantageous in the sense that they are relatively inexpensive and time-efficient. Additionally, the richest information stems from respondents as they have access to their thoughts, feelings and behaviours. The most widely used and well validated personality measures available are:

- NEO Personality Inventory 3 (NEO-PI-3)
- Personality Assessment Inventory
- Millon Clinical Multiaxial Inventory (MCMII)
- Minnesota Multiphasic Personality Inventory – 2 Restructured Form (MMPI-2-RF)

NEO personality inventory 3

The NEO Personality Inventory is a well-established 240-item comprehensive and detailed assessment of adult and adolescent personality, based upon the major domains of the Five-Factor Model of Personality (Costa and McCrae 2010a;b). In addition to measuring neuroticism, extraversion, openness, agreeableness and conscientiousness, NEO-PI-3 offers a further insight into the six facets that define each domain. The test can be administered in 30–40 minutes. Separate versions are available for adolescents (12–20 years old) and adults (21+ years old). This latest version of the NEO-PI has revised certain items to lower the reading level necessary to complete the measure, thus making it more attainable for those with lower educational levels.

Personality assessment inventory

The Personality Assessment Inventory (PAI) is a 344-item self-report measure. The PAI has verified reliability and validity in assessing personality and psychopathology in various settings including clinical and non-clinical populations (Charnas et al. 2010). It contains a Treatment Rejection Scale (RXR) and a PAI treatment process Index (TPI) which identify several factors that are associated with treatment amenability and motivation. In some cases, a brief and valid assessment of psychopathology and personality can be beneficial, particularly where a comprehensive assessment is impractical due to costs and time restraints. The Personality Assessment Screener (PAS) is a 22-item self-report measure of the Personality Assessment Inventory (PAI). The PAS identifies respondents who would likely achieve a clinically significant PAI personality profile. Charnas and colleagues examined the validity of the PAS and found it was a valid measure, which indicated clinically significant PAI profiles amongst American soldiers.

Minnesota multiphasic personality inventory – 2 restructured form (MMPI-2-RF)

The Minnesota Multiphasic Personality Inventory (MMPI) assessments including the original MMPI, the MMPI-2 and the MMPI-2 Restructured Form (MMPI-2-RF) were developed to assess a broad range of personality and psychopathological characteristics. The MMPI is widely used to assess personality and psychopathology in mental health settings (Nelson et al. 2014). The MMPI-2 and MMPI-2-RF have demonstrated utility in identifying psychopathology and the treatment needs of clients (Nelson et al. 2014). The MMPI-2-RF is the latest version of the MMPI (Ben-Porath 2012). The MMPI-2 RF comprises 51 scales that measure validity, interpersonal difficulties, personality pathology, and psychopathology, somatic and cognitive difficulties (Tarescavage et al. 2013). There is substantial empirical evidence indicating that the MMPI-2-RF has adequate reliability and validity across various settings (Gervais et al. 2011; Tarescavage et al. 2013) and is a reliable tool to assess suicide risk (Gervais et al. 2011). The assessment of suicide risk is an important aspect of the MMPI-2-RF given the strong association between personality disorders and suicide risks.

Millon clinical multiaxial inventory (MCMII)

The MCMII is one of the most widely used personality assessments in clinical settings. The MCMII is intended for use with people who are hypothesised to be exhibiting personality pathology; it is not intended to be used with a non-clinical population (Millon et al. 2012). The MCMII comprises 175 items that are collapsed into 24 clinical scales and three modifier scales (Disclosure, Desirability and Debasement). The modifier scales assess a respondent's tendency to over/under report difficulties and respond in a socially desirable manner. The first section of the MCMII personality profile contains information on the severity of personality disorders ranging from masochistic to schizoid, the second section represents severe personality disorders, the schizotypal, paranoid and borderline. The other two sections relate to Axis I disorders ranging from moderate clinical syndromes such as anxiety and dysthymia to more severe syndromes such as major depression, post-traumatic stress disorder and thought disorder (Craig 2013). Examination of the MCMII personality profile highlights the relationship between interpersonal style, adaptive coping behaviour, symptoms and personality structure (Craig 2013).

Limitations of personality assessment

Aside from the obvious pitfalls of self-report measures such as social desirability bias and over- or under-estimation of one's tendencies, personality assessments are also largely subject to the impact of the client's current emotional state. It is logical to assume that if one is attending a psychologist or other mental health professional, their emotional state is somewhat compromised, thus preventing them from providing an accurate description of their typical way of thinking, behaving, feeling and relating to others. The impact of states on traits is illustrated by the change in prevalence rates of personality disorders reported in The Collaborative Longitudinal study of personality disorders. This study found that 14% of people who met all diagnostic criteria for borderline personality disorder at the outset, fulfilled only two of the diagnostic criteria at six-month follow up. Moreover, 11% of these cases were considered to have a remission from a personality disorder, which was attributed to psychological difficulties being resolved (Gunderson et al. 2003). An alternative explanation for this remission is the inaccurate assessment of personality disorder due to the presence of psychological distress.

Various psychological disorders have cognitive and motivational dimensions which may impact the validity of the personality assessment (Shedler et al. 2014). For example, people may over-report their difficulties as a means of communicating their need for help which could confound the personality assessment results. In essence, the crossover effect of states on traits coupled with misrepresentations stemming from cognitive and motivational biases are an inevitable aspect of personality assessment and must be considered when interpreting the results.

KEY POINT

Current emotional state can influence responses in personality assessment.

Integrating personality into formulation

The information obtained from initial assessment and therapeutic dialogue should be utilised to co-construct a comprehensive and meaningful formulation for the client. To truly encapsulate personal meaning within the formulation, the practitioner is encouraged to extract relevant information on how the client's personality developed, how it relates to their difficulties and even how it has helped them to manage and overcome psychological distress in the past. There are a number of key indicators expressed through the therapeutic dialogue that would suggest that personality traits are associated with the client's difficulties. These indicators can be considered across three main categories; historical, current and dynamic factors.

Historical

The historical factors that should be incorporated into a formulation and discussed within the therapeutic dialogue include poor attainment of life goals, poor relating with others across various situations, early trauma and a disruption of relationships with primary caregivers (Charnas et al. 2010; McWilliams 2011).

Current

Current factors refer to the client's presenting difficulties and often include multiple complex issues and unexplained physical symptoms. The practitioner should focus on topics including current interpersonal relationships and coping styles.

Dynamic

The dynamic factors relate to difficulty developing a therapeutic relationship, frequent rupture and repair, poor boundaries in therapy and transference and counter-transference. This can be considered a part of the client's *internal* therapeutic dialogue, as compared to their *external* dialogue which would include discussions of their historical and current factors as described above.

Through carefully crafted and monitored dialogue, the practitioner should convey an understanding of the person's difficulties and explore the impact of the client's personality on their psychological distress. If maladaptive personality traits are evident, the practitioner should convey the idea that part of the client's personality has developed as a coping mechanism to assist the client cope with aversive experiences. The link between the historical, contextual and dynamic factors can be highlighted to the client in order to enhance their understanding of their own personality and the impact of their personality on their micro and macro environment. This, aside from a reduction in symptomology, is a primary goal of therapy – the development of an assisted environment, conducive to a learning experience, where the client can become a student of their personality factors and structures that generated both reactions and responses from their everyday environment.

An exploration of the results can often stimulate a reflective discussion about facets of the client's personality, how it may have been contributing to their difficulties, how it may present some challenges for them, but also how it may be utilised as a strength in its own right. For example, an extremely conscientious client may have problems with spontaneity or be prone to perfectionism. However, it can be explained that because of this, they are also more likely to carry out therapeutic tasks and reflective homework, thus heightening therapeutic engagement and increasing their chances of eliciting successful change. Regardless of the client's compilation of personality traits, the practitioner should focus on emphasising the positive aspects and mitigating the negative aspects of their personality style. Relating personality to socially significant aspects of behaviour can provide some very valuable information for the client, and may shed some light on the characteristic way in which they think, feel, behave and relate to themselves and others. The subsequent integration of this information into the formulation enhances personal meaning and context throughout the process for the client.

KEY POINT

Personality traits do not necessarily consist of better or worse features; they are only better or worse to the extent they relate to situations and circumstances.

Transference and counter-transference

It is recommended that transference and countertransference are incorporated into the formulation process, although this is an area often overlooked by psychologists (British Psychological Society 2011). Counter-transference (a psychologist's emotional response to a client) is viewed as a source of valuable diagnostic and therapeutic information and, when used correctly, can play a crucial role in the therapy process and outcome. A number of psychodynamic models propose that the clinician's inner experience partially stems from the patient's inner world and can be utilised to understand the client's difficulties. From this perspective, considering the psychologist's response to the client's personality and interpersonal functioning when formulating has relevance for managing the therapeutic process and tailoring the intervention appropriately. A number of studies have investigated the relationship between personality disorders and clinicians' emotional experiences. Rossberg et al. (2007) found that the DSM personality clusters A and B elicited more negative countertransference in clinicians compared to cluster C. In line with these findings, a more recent study found that borderline personality disorder was related with helpless/inadequate, overwhelmed/disorganized and overinvolved/special countertransference in clinicians whilst paranoid and anti-social personality disorders were associated with criticised/mistreated countertransference (Lingiardi et al. 2015).

In essence, psychological formulations inevitably arise from and are influenced by the clinician's professional and personal experiences, beliefs and assumptions. As such, psychologists need to develop reflexivity and self-awareness in order to ensure a transparent and appropriate formulation that is based on the client's personal experience and reflects their inner world, rather than the psychologist's biases (British Psychological Society 2011). Through the therapeutic dialogue, the practitioner should convey an understanding of the person's difficulties and explore the impact of the client's personality on their psychological distress. The link between the historical, contextual and dynamic factors should be highlighted to the client in order to enhance their understanding of their own personality and the impact of their personality on their immediate psychosocial environment. Aside from reducing symptomology, facilitating clients to gain a deeper understanding of how they think, feel and behave in response to their environment is ultimately a primary goal of therapy.

Conclusion

The development of personality and its influence on psychological well-being is complex and multi-faceted. Research confirms that personality influences not only the development of psychological distress but also how this distress is expressed. Certain personality traits are implicated in the development of a number of psychological disorders including substance abuse, PTSD and eating disorders. The assessment of personality is a dynamic and organic process, continually adapting and changing as the therapeutic relationship evolves and new knowledge arises in the various professional encounters. In order to ensure an integrative reflexive approach, the practitioner can usefully consider the impact that a client's personality has on the professional encounter and hypothesise what this may add to understanding their distress. Rather than defining the person solely by their difficulties or symptoms, integrating personality factors into a formulation ensures that a comprehensive account of the person is generated and enhances understanding of distress, coping strategies, strengths, goals and aspirations.

Reflective exercise

Complete a measure of personality that is well-established, well researched and has strong reliability and validity norms.

a.   Score the measure and consider how your scores fall on each trait compared to standardised norms.
b.   How accurate is the representation of your personality and your experience of life to date?
c.   Are there any scores that surprise you?
d.   Consider how you would like this information to be relayed back to you, if you were the client.
e.   Identify one way in which your score for each trait may have helped you to cope with a life experience, and one way in which it may have impeded you or contributed to distress. In other words, consider the pros and cons of your score on each trait.
f.   Consider how this new knowledge may contribute to an increased understanding of yourself in the future.

REFERENCES

Anaya, B., & Pérez-Edgar, K. 2018. Personality development in the context of individual traits and parenting dynamics. *New Ideas in Psychology*. (Online only) doi:10.1016/j.newideapsych.2018.03.002

Ansell, E. B., Wright, A. G., Markowitz, J. C., Sanislow, C. A., Hopwood, C. J., Zanarini, M. C., Yen, S., Pinto, A., McGlashan, T. H., & Grilo, C. M. 2015. Personality disorder risk factors for suicide attempts over 10 years of follow-up. *Personality Disorders: Theory, Research, and Treatment*, 6(2), 161.

Asendorpf, J. B., Denissen, J. J. A., & van Aken, M. A. G. 2008. Inhibited and aggressive preschool children at 23 years of age: Personality and social transitions into adulthood. *Developmental Psychology*, 44(4), 997–1011.

Bender, D. S., Dolan, R. T., Skodol, A. E., Sanislow, C. A., Dyck, I. R., McGlashan, T. H., McGlashan, Shea, M. T., Zanarini, M. C., Oldham, J. M., & Gunderson, J. G. 2014. Treatment utilization by patients with personality disorders. *American Journal of Psychiatry*, 158(2), 295–302.

Ben-Porath, Y. S. 2012. Addressing challenges to MMPI-2-RF-based testimony: Questions and answers. *Archives of Clinical Neuropsychology*, 27, 1–15.

Blasco-Fontecilla, H., Peñas-Lledó, E., Vaquero-Lorenzo, C., Dorado, P., Saiz-Ruiz, J., Llerena, A. & Baca-García, E. 2014. CYP2D6 polymorphism and mental and personality disorders in suicide attempters. *Journal of Personality Disorders*, 28(6), 873–883.

British Psychological Society. 2011. Division of Clinical Psychology. Good Practice Guidelines on the Use of Psychological Formulation, [online], available: https://www.canterbury.ac.uk/social-and-applied-sciences/salomons-centre-for-applied-psychology/docs/resources/DCP-Guidelines-for-Formulation.pdf [accessed 18 September 2015].

Calkins, S. D. 2010. Commentary: Conceptual and methodological challenges to the study of emotion regulation and psychopathology. *Journal of Psychopathology and Behavioral Assessment*, 32(1), 92–95.

Carleton, R. N., Mulvogue, M. K., & Duranceau, S. 2015. PTSD personality subtypes in women exposed to intimate-partner violence. *Psychological Trauma: Theory, Research, Practice, and Policy*, 7(2), 154.

Carr, A., & McNulty, M. 2006. *The Handbook of Adult Clinical Psychology: An Evidence-Based Practice Approach*. London: Routledge.

Carver, C. S. & Connor-Smith, J. 2010. Personality and coping. *Annual Review of Psychology*, 61, 679–704.

Cassin, S. E., & von Ranson, K. M. 2005. Personality and eating disorders: A decade in review. *Clinical Psychology Reviews*, 25(7), 895–916.

Castillo, H. S., Paz-Trejo, D., Ramírez, J. V., González, P. Z., & Migliaro, M. 2014. Neurobiology of Posttraumatic Stress Disorder (PTSD) and its frontostriatal implications: A short review. *Actualidades En Psicología*, 28(117), 13–20.

Cattell, R. B. 1957. *Personality and Motivation Structure and Measurement*. Oxford, England: World Book Co.

Charnas, J. W., Hilsenroth, M. J., Zodan, J., & Blais, M. A. 2010. Should I stay or should I go? Personality assessment inventory and Rorschach indices of early withdrawal from psychotherapy. *Psychotherapy: Theory, Research, Practice, Training*, 47(4), 484.

Coleman, J., & Trunzo, J. 2015. Personality, social stress, and drug use among college students. *Psi Chi Journal of Psychological Research*, 20(1), 52–56.

Costa, P. T., & McCrae, R. R. 2010a. Bridging the gap with the five-factor model. *Personality Disorders: Theory, Research, and Treatment*, 1, 127–130.

Costa, P. T., & McCrae, R. R. 2010b. *The NEO Personality Inventory: 3*. Odessa, Florida: Psychological assessment resources.

Craig, R. J. 2013. *The Millon Clinical Multiaxial Inventory: A Clinical Research Information Synthesis*. New Jersey: Routledge.

Daspe, M. È., Sabourin, S., Lussier, Y., Péloquin, K., & Wright, J. 2015. Is the association between sexual satisfaction and neuroticism in treatment-seeking couples curvilinear? *Couple and Family Psychology: Research and Practice*, 4(2), 92.

Daspe, M. È., Sabourin, S., Péloquin, K., Lussier, Y., & Wright, J. 2013. Curvilinear associations between neuroticism and dyadic adjustment in treatment-seeking couples. *Journal of Family Psychology*, 27(2), 232.

Eysenck, S. B. G., & Eysenck, H. J. 1963. The validity of questionnaire and rating assessments of extraversion and neuroticism, and their factorial stability. *British Journal of Psychology*, 54(1), 51–62.

Friedman, H. S., Kern, M. L., & Reynolds, C. A. 2010. Personality and health, subjective well-being, and longevity. *Journal of Personality*, 78(1), 179–216.

Gervais, R. O., Wygant, D. B., Sellbom, M., & Ben-Porath, Y. S. 2011. Associations between symptom validity test failure and scores on the MMPI-2-RF validity and substantive scales. *Journal of Personality Assessment*, 93(5), 508–517.

Gunderson, J. G., Bender, D., Sanislow, C., Yen S., Rettew, J. B., Dolan-Sewellb, R., Dyck, I. et al. 2003. Plausibility and possible determinants of sudden "remissions" in borderline patients. *Psychiatry*, 66(2), 111–119.

Hasin, D., Fenton, M. C., Skodol, A., Krueger, R., Keyes, K., Geier, T., Greenstein, E., Blanco, C., & Grant, B. 2011. Personality disorders and the 3-year course of alcohol, drug, and nicotine use disorders. *Archives of General Psychiatry*, 68(11), 1158–1167.

Hopwood, C. J., Baker, K. L., & Morey, L. C. 2008. Extratest validity of selected personality assessment inventory scales and indicators in an inpatient substance abuse setting. *Journal of Personality Assessment*, 90(6), 574–577.

Kim, S., & Kochanska, G. 2012. Child temperament moderates effects of parent–child mutuality on self-regulation: A relationship-based path for emotionally negative infants. *Child Development*, 83(4), 1275–1289.

Lahey, B. B. 2009. Public health significance of neuroticism. *American Psychologist*, 64(4), 241.

Lingiardi, V., Tanzilli, A., & Colli, A. 2015. Does the severity of psychopathological symptoms mediate the relationship between patient personality and therapist response? *Psychotherapy*, 52(2), 228.

McAdams, D. P., & Olson, B. D. 2010. Personality development: Continuity and change. *Annual Review of Psychology*, 61, 517–542.

McCrae, R. R., & Costa, P. T., Jr. 2008. The five-factor theory of personality. In O. P. John, R. W. Robins, & L. A. Pervin (eds.), *Handbook of Personality: Theory and Research* (pp. 159–181). New York, NY, US: Guilford Press.

McWilliams, N. 2011. *Psychoanalytic Diagnosis: Understanding Personality Structure in the Clinical Process*. New York: Guilford Press.

Miller, J. D., Gentile, B., & Campbell, W. K. 2013. A test of the construct validity of the five-factor narcissism inventory. *Journal of Personality Assessment*, 95(4), 377–387.

Millon, T., Millon, C. M., Meagher, S., Grossman, S., & Ramnath, R. 2012. *Personality Disorders in Modern Life*. Hoboken, New Jersey: John Wiley & Sons.

Mommersteeg, P. M., Denollet, J., Kavelaars, A., Geuze, E., Vermetten, E., & Heijnen, C. J. 2011. Type D personality, temperament, and mental health in military personnel awaiting deployment. *International Journal of Behavioral Medicine*, 18(2), 131–138.

Nelson, N. W., Anderson, C. R., Hoelzle, J. B., & Arbisi, P. A. 2014. Psychological assessment of veterans in outpatient mental health settings. In S. S. Bush (ed.), *Psychological Assessment of Veterans* (pp. 17–50). Oxford: Oxford University Press.

Reitz, A. K., Zimmermann, J., Hutteman, R., Specht, J., & Neyer, F. J. 2014. How peers make a difference: The role of peer groups and peer relationships in personality development. *European Journal of Personality*, 28, 279–288.

Rossberg, J. I., Karterud, S., Pedersen, G., & Friis, S. 2007. An empirical study of countertransference reactions towards patients with personality disorders. *Comprehensive Psychiatry*, 48, 225–230.

Shedler, J., Beck, A., Fonagy, P., Gabbard, G. O., Gunderson, J., Kernberg, O., & Westen, D. 2014. Personality disorders in DSM-5. *American Journal of Psychiatry Journal*, 167(9), 1026–1028.

Skodol, A. E., Bender, D. S., & Morey, L. C. 2014. Narcissistic personality disorder in DSM-5. *Personality Disorders: Theory, Research, and Treatment*, 5(4), 422.

Syed, M., & Seiffge-Krenke, I. 2013. Personality development from adolescence to emerging adulthood: Linking trajectories of ego development to the family context and identity formation. *Journal of Personality and Social Psychology*, 104, 371–384.

Tarescavage, A. M., Wygant, D. B., Boutacoff, L. I., & Ben-Porath, Y. S. 2013. Reliability, validity, and utility of the Minnesota Multiphasic Personality Inventory-2-Restructured Form (MMPI-2-RF) in assessments of bariatric surgery candidates. *Psychological Assessment*, 25(4), 1179.

Thomas, A., & Chess, S. 1977. *Temperament and Development*. New York: Brunner/ Mazel.

Watson, D., & Casillas, A. 2003. Neuroticism: Adaptive and maladaptive features. In E. C. Chang, & L. J. Sanna (eds.), *Virtue, Vice, and Personality: The Complexity of Behaviour* (pp. 145–161). Washington, DC: American Psychological Association.

Wedig, M. M., Silverman, M. H., Frankenburg, F. R., Reich, D. B., Fitzmaurice, G., & Zanarini, M. C. 2012. Predictors of suicide attempts in patients with borderline personality disorder over 16 years of prospective follow-up. *Psychological Medicine*, 42(11), 2395–2404.

Widiger, T. A. 2011. Personality and psychopathology. *World Psychiatry*, 10(2), 103–106.

Chapter 6

Sleep

Kristina Cahill, Julie Lynch, and Patrick Ryan

CHAPTER TOPICS

- Fundamental characteristics of sleep including stages, optimal duration and regularity
- Relationship between sleep and cognitive and emotional processing
- Sleep and mental health: a causal factor or just a correlation?
- Successfully integrating information on sleep into clinical interview

Introduction

Sleep is a fundamental part of daily routine, with the majority of individuals spending approximately one third of their lives in this state (Killgore 2010). While the exact biological purpose may remain a mystery (Assefa, Diaz-Abad, Wickwire and Scharf, 2015), scientists agree that sleep plays a vital role in brain function and is deeply embedded within the various processes that contribute to our everyday functioning, across many body systems that lead to the restoration of the body and brain. Numerous factors can contribute to sleep disruption, including lifestyle, environmental factors and specific medical conditions, with adverse short and long-term consequences for the individual involved. A highly complex, bidirectional relationship between sleep and mental health has been widely documented in the literature. Despite this, information on sleep remains largely excluded from traditional psychological formulation. More recently however, experts in the field have started to recognise that sleep disruption is a neglected factor that contributes to the instigation or maintenance of mental health issues, and that sleep has "powerful diagnostic and therapeutic potential that we are yet to fully understand or make use of" (Walker, 2017, p. 150).

The process of clinical formulation aims to provide a psychological understanding of a person's difficulties and generally act as a guide for the clinician towards a particular intervention plan to help address these difficulties (Brown and Völlm 2013). Despite this core skill being considered the 'bread and butter' of mental health practitioners particularly in the field of psychology, clinicians can tend to approach case formulation with some apprehension, as it can be a struggle to assimilate substantial quantities of information into a coherent workable, framework. Upon examination of the traditional models of formulation (i.e., behavioural, psychodynamic and systemic), it becomes clear that the emphasis in each approach varies and relies on different information from the clinical assessment. In cognitive behavioural approaches, constructing a formulation focuses on presenting, precipitating, perpetuating, predisposing and protective factors (Dudley and Kuyken 2014). The psychodynamic perspective focuses on a combination of the dynamic, developmental, structural and adaptive patterns in which individuals approach inner conflict (Leiper 2014). Finally, the systemic perspective constructs a formulation around the nature of the interpersonal interactions between the individual and their wider systems, particularly the family system (Dallos and Stedmon 2014). Although each have their own merits and relevance for how to approach an individual case, they are also limited in terms of the boundaries they place on what type of information is incorporated into the formulation. Information that may be integral to understanding a person's difficulties (e.g., sleep patterns and disruptions) may be lost, greatly reducing the practitioner's capacity to generate a comprehensive profile of the individual and their difficulties, thus limiting important opportunities for intervention.

The characteristics of sleep will be offered from the outset to provide sufficient context to subsequent sections of this chapter. Following this, the complex relationship between sleep and cognitive and emotional health will be discussed under headings such as memory, learning, insight, inhibition, decision making and emotional processing. The chapter offers a thorough review of the literature that explores whether sleep difficulties are a causal factor for various psychological disorders, or whether they are, in fact, symptoms associated with these disorders. Most importantly, the reader will be navigated through some practical ways in which they might examine their client's sleeping patterns in clinical assessment, both informally by incorporating pertinent open-ended questions into therapeutic dialogue and formally, by using psychometric measures.

Characteristics of sleep

Sleep is a biological process that is fundamental to optimal health. It plays a critical role in brain function and consequently, mental health. What follows is a review of specific sleep stages, the neurological processes underlying circadian rhythms and the characteristics of normal, healthy sleep such as duration, quality, timing and regularity.

Stages of sleep

Researchers have identified two basic types of sleep; rapid eye movement (REM) sleep and non-rapid eye movement (NREM) sleep. Until recently, it was believed that NREM sleep progressed through four 'stages', each stage characterised by increasing sleep depth (Institute of Medicine 2006). The American Academy of Sleep Medicine have since developed a refined sleep classification system

Table 6.1 Fast facts on sleep

Stage 1 NREM sleep

- Short stage between wakefulness and sleep
- Very light, easily disrupted sleep
- Breathing regulates and heart rate slows
- Represents about 5% of total adult sleep time

Stage 2 NREM sleep

- First unequivocal stage of sleep
- Conscious awareness of outside world begins to fade completely
- Constitutes approx. 50% of total adult sleep time

Stage 3 NREM sleep

- Known as deep sleep, or slow-wave sleep (SWS)
- Represents approx. 15%–20% of total adult sleep time
- Difficult to waken somebody during this stage
- Muscles relax, supply of blood to muscles increase, body repairs and grows tissue
- Hormones are released, energy stores are replenished

REM sleep

- Accounts for approx. 20%–25% of an adult's sleep cycle
- Blood pressure and heart rate increases
- Eyes move rapidly from side to side behind closed eyelids
- Brain wave activity becomes closer to that observed in wakefulness
- Most dreams occur during REM sleep
- REM sleep is thought to aid in memory consolidation
- Drinking alcohol before bed reduces the amount of REM sleep

with only three stages of NREM sleep (Table 6.1). A cycle of sleep constitutes a progression of sleep stages from NREM1, to NREM 2 and NREM 3, finishing with REM sleep. A good quality of sleep consists of five or six of these cycles, whereas poor quality sleep typically consists of fewer. Each cycle lasts approximately 1.5 hours and all four stages need to occur in order to wake up feeling rested.

KEY POINT

Patterns of sleep are broadly influenced by environmental factors that are often within the client's control, representing discrete opportunities for intervention.

Sleep duration

The National Sleep Foundation (NSF) recommends 7–9 hours of sleep per night for adults aged between 18 years and 64 years. This fluctuates depending on age range, with younger children requiring more, and older adults requiring marginally less. Surveys conducted in recent years would suggest that the reality for many people is far from ideal however. One third of Irish adults are getting fewer than six hours of sleep a night (O'Brien 2017). 35% of Americans get fewer than 7 hours of sleep per night (Centers for Disease Control and Prevention 2016).

Timing and regularity

Despite the common emphasis placed on sufficient sleeping hours, sleep is a multi-dimensional concept and more recently, it has been recognised that its importance to optimal health and functioning may not be entirely dependent on duration. Researchers in the USA have suggested that the *regularity* of sleep (i.e., going to sleep and waking up at approximately the same time every day) may be just as important as the number of hours spent sleeping (Phillips et al. 2017). Phillips and colleagues demonstrated that students with less regular sleep patterns produced poorer grades and were able to predict a daily mood score based upon the regularity of the student's sleep pattern over the past week. The importance of a regular sleep pattern can be better understood by examining the impact of regularity on REM and NREM cycles, as described above.

REM and NREM cycles are largely regulated by circadian rhythm, which is an individual's internal biological clock. This clock operates on a 24-hour cycle and is largely responsible for overseeing our sleeping and waking times. When a regular sleeping pattern has been established, circadian rhythm functions at an optimal level. For example, an important function of circadian rhythm is to ensure that certain hormones are released approximately one hour before waking, thus gently preparing the body for wakefulness and the day ahead. Night shift workers often struggle with falling asleep when they go to bed and staying awake while at work, because their natural circadian rhythm and sleep-wake cycle is disrupted.

Role of sleep in cognitive functioning

The relationship between thinking and feeling is well established, thus the role of sleep in cognitive functioning is worth considering here. The impact of sleep on cognition has predominantly been examined in the context of sleep deprivation and restriction, with reviews and meta-analyses documenting correlations between disrupted sleep and cognitive deficits in the areas of executive attention, working memory, processing speed, reasoning, sensory perception, learning, inhibitory control and decision making (Lim and Dinges 2010; Killgore 2010).

Sleep, memory and learning

Research has shown that sleep is essential for the processes involved before and after learning occurs, namely encoding, integration and consolidation of information (Diekelmann and Born 2010). Poe et al. (2014) also examined the functional role of sleep in learning and memory paying attention to the underlying processes of

REM and non-REM sleep, and how they influenced learning and memory. Their study proposed that during REM sleep, a specific neural environment occurs whereby synaptic remodeling and growth can take place. Other studies have shown that synaptic remodeling and plasticity is associated with consolidation of information within memory (Geinisman et al. 2000; Bailey and Kandel 2008). Poe et al. linked these patterns of synaptic plasticity, namely long-term potentiation (the strengthening of synapses increasing transmission between synapses); with increased activity in the hippocampus during REM sleep. Their results suggested that REM sleep deprivation is linked to poor consolidation of information.

Sleep and insight

Research has examined how individuals consolidate newly learned or experienced impressions during sleep, and to what extent this information is reprocessed and restructured during sleep. This form of mental restructuring that leads to an increase of knowledge and awareness involves a level of insight, which can be defined as the capacity of the individual to gain an accurate and deep understanding and awareness of something, someone or themselves (Sternberg and Davidson 1996). From a psychological perspective, insight has been described as a form of wisdom and a 'view under the surface, an understanding of a person from within and resonance on outer events (Moro et al. 2012, p. 354). It is considered a vital aspect of psychotherapy, as the therapeutic process aims to cultivate a personal understanding within the client, of events and emotions from different points in their life.

Sleep has been associated with the gaining or increasing of insight. Research indicates that sleep facilitates consolidation of memories (Maquet 2001), and has generated the hypothesis that insight during sleep can restructure how the memory or information is represented, which subsequently facilitates more insightful behaviour. A study to test this idea was conducted by Wagner et al. (2004). Participants were placed into sleep deprivation and nocturnal sleep subgroups following initial task representation. When tested, twice as many participants who had slept gained insight into the abstract rule of the task when compared with those who were sleep deprived. These results indicated that the restructuring of memories is instigated by an effect of sleep that differs from underlying procedural motor learning, and with amplification during sleep, can lead to more implicit memory representation, resulting in more insightful behaviour.

This link between sleep and insight has been in the context of emotional memories. Payne and Kensinger (2012) provided evidence that sleep has highly selective effects on emotional memory consolidation, with a preference for preserving the more emotionally salient aspects of complex experiences. They found that after information is encoded in memory, it undergoes an 'offline period of consolidation' that occurs during sleep, and that a single night of sleep involved processes that incite changes in emotional memory retrieval and how it is represented. More recently, Payne and Kensinger (2018) connected negative emotional memory formation with sleep to show how an individual consolidates negative aspects of an emotional event. Both studies highlight the importance of sleep in consolidating emotional memories as a necessary proponent for how an individual makes sense and gathers meaning and insight from their experiences.

Sleep, inhibition and decision making

Examining the impact of sleep on other aspects of executive functioning, research highlights how inhibition, decision making and risk taking are affected through disrupted sleep. Venkatraman et al. (2007) examined how short-term sleep deprivation influenced decision-making processes using functional neuroimaging. A link was found between sleep deprivation and greater activation in the right nucleus accumbens (brain region associated with risky decision making and emotional processing), when participants were asked to make a choice based on reward. The authors proposed that sleep deprivation was directly linked with elevated expectations of reward and a reduced response to losses following risky decision making, suggesting that competent decision making when faced with sleep deprivation is comprised. Other research has reported that even the loss of a single night's sleep leads to increased impulsivity, particularly with regard to negative stimuli, such that sleep deprivation increases disinhibited responses, and can even lead to a diminished response to positive stimuli (Zohar et al. 2005). The results from the Anderson and Platten (2011) study indicated that sleep deprivation can lead to enhanced impulsivity to negative emotional stimuli, and losing one night's sleep can lead to a deficit in response inhibition.

Role of sleep in emotional processing

The well-established relationship between emotional and cognitive processes and the detrimental effect of sleep deprivation on cognitive abilities contributed to the proposition that the processing and evaluation of emotional stimuli is also adversely affected by sleep deprivation (Killgore 2010; Tempesta et al. 2010). Neuroimaging studies have shown that sleep deprivation can reduce activation of the medial prefrontal cortex, the amygdala (brain regions associated with emotional processing) and the functional connectivity between both during emotional processing such as emotion recognition (Van Der Helm et al. 2010; Gujar et al. 2011). Researchers examined how insufficient sleep affected an individual's emotional intelligence and constructive thinking, given how necessary they were for adaptive functioning. Sleep deprivation was associated with lower emotional intelligence and reductions in self-regard, assertiveness, independence and self-actualisation (Killgore et al. 2008). Such results have practical implications for how clients manage negative feelings and stress, as well as how they relate to others. In concurrence with the results of Venkatraman et al. (2007), this study also found a link between sleep deprivation, poor impulse control and difficulty with delayed gratification.

There is much empirical evidence documenting how emotion is processed during disrupted sleep, but also how it is expressed in terms of mood. Studies have shown that among the many side effects or symptoms associated with sleep deprivation, the detrimental influence of fatigue on mood is one of the more significant effects. Scott et al. (2006) found a strong correlation between sleep deprivation, subjective vigour and depression when tested in the general functioning population. Similarly, with individuals whose occupation involves night shift work or disrupted sleeping patterns (e.g., emergency department staff) there is an abundance of evidence to suggest that both the quality and quantity of sleep is linked with negative mood disturbances, depression and burnout (Friedman, Bigger and Kornfeld 1971; Samkoff and Jacques 1991; Rosen et al. 2006). A recent review of the literature has suggested that disrupted sleep is a major causal factor in the development of depression (Meerlo et al. 2015). Further studies have highlighted that self-reports of recurring sleep problems are associated with symptoms of anxiety and depression, with increased frequency of disturbance associated with increased severity of symptoms (Tkachenko et al. 2014).

KEY POINT

Adults whose occupation involves shift work or extremely varied work schedules are particularly susceptible to sleep problems.

Causation or correlation?

Thus far, the chapter has established how sleep is linked with a variety of different but interconnected bodily functions such as cognitive and emotional processing. When exploring the nature of the relationship between sleep and mental health, it is evident that positive affect and well-being have been directly correlated with good sleep, and good sleep has even been described as a 'buffering agent' for impact of psychological risk factors (Steptoe et al. 2008). With this view in mind, it is plausible to suggest a strong link between disrupted sleep and mental health difficulties. What appears to be the point of contention however, is whether sleep problems are a causal factor for various psychological disorders, or whether they are, in fact, symptoms associated with these disorders?

Rationale for causation

Insomnia (defined as a disorder where people have trouble either falling asleep or staying asleep) has been described as a risk factor and a gateway for poor mental health. A meta-analysis by Riemann and Voderholzer (2003) sought to establish whether chronic insomnia could predict the development of depression, strictly controlling for any psychiatric history. Researchers found that insomnia at baseline acted as a predictive factor for increased risk of developing depression. A more recent longitudinal study by Gregory et al. (2005) indicated that persistent sleep problems in childhood acted as a significant predictive factor for the development of anxiety in adulthood.

Looking beyond affective disorders, there is evidence pointing to a link between disrupted sleep and an increased risk of developing post-traumatic stress disorder (PTSD), schizophrenia and substance abuse, among others. Although disrupted sleep has not necessarily been termed as a prerequisite for the development of PTSD, it has been suggested that sleep problems such as nightmares, night terrors and persistent awakenings post-trauma can exacerbate the onset of PTSD (Spoormaker and Montgomery 2008). Sleep disturbance has also been identified as a contributing factor for the development of psychosis, due to the impact of sleep abnormalities and disrupted circadian rhythm cycles on the development of schizophrenia (Ruhrmann et al. 2010; Wilson and Argyropoulos 2012). Finally, another longitudinal study found that sleep problems in early childhood acted as a significant marker for the subsequent onset of alcohol and drug problems in adulthood (Wong et al. 2004). While this particular study did not examine the underlying mechanisms of this correlation in great depth, the authors suggested the link between sleeping difficulties and cognitive deficits may result in a psychological and cognitive vulnerabilities which (coupled with negative environmental factors) could lead to a higher risk of exposure to drugs or alcohol. Another potential explanation is the likelihood of an individual's increased dependence on drugs and alcohol as a method of coping with sleeping difficulties.

Rationale for correlation

The other face of the coin posits that disrupted sleep and insomnia could be considered as symptoms of an overarching psychological disorder. Considering that significantly disrupted sleep is part of the diagnostic criteria for major depressive disorder (as well as a number of other psychological disorders) under both DSM-5 and ICD-11, it is understandable how sleep may be viewed as part of the problem, rather than part of the wider cause. Studies have outlined a significant increase in sleep disturbances following the development of a psychological disorders such as affective disorders (Staner et al. 2006), schizophrenia (Ritsner et al. 2004), PTSD (Lavie 2001) and bipolar disorder (Harvey et al. 2009). In individuals who suffer with chronic somatoform pain, Aigner et al. (2003) reported a high prevalence rate of sleep disturbances in this particular population. Recommendations from this particular study include that sleep be considered a prominent factor in the formulation process regarding the persistence and aggravation of chronic pain, as sleep deprivation produces hyperalgesic changes within the body that can heighten sensitivity to the experience of pain.

Although sleep disturbances are not included as part of the diagnostic criteria for various personality disorders, there is a growing body of evidence suggesting that individuals with borderline personality disorder (BPD) experience a variety of difficulties in both the quantity and quality of their sleep (Selby 2013). A possible explanation for this link could be that interpersonal difficulties and emotional dysregulation during the daytime could lead to increased rumination, particularly at periods such as bedtime, where the mind has little to no distraction from such ruminations. This constant rumination could lead to difficulty initiating and maintaining sleep and increased daytime fatigue.

A compromise

A third view, and possibly the most likely, proposes that the relationship between sleep and mental health difficulties is more complex and inter-related than simple cause-and-effect. There is an abundance of evidence to suggest that sleep disturbances could act as both a precursor to and a result of various mental health difficulties. The Maastricht Ageing Study (MAAS) explored whether sleep complaints in middle-aged and older adults predicted global cognitive decline over a period of three years. Researchers found that sleep complaints were negatively associated with cognitive performance, but more interestingly, the association between sleep complaints and cognitive decline disappeared once depression was controlled for (Jelicic et al. 2002). This begs the question of whether poor quality of sleep leads directly to poor cognitive function, or whether poor sleep causes an increase in depressive symptoms which subsequently results in cognitive decline.

With disrupted sleep and mental health issues forming a vicious, bidirectional cycle, it can be difficult to separate one from the other when focusing on the individual. To use the results of the Selby (2013) study on BPD as an example, it is plausible to suggest that the interpersonal difficulties associated with borderline personality traits can increase vulnerability to sleep disturbance, but also conversely, the consequences of poor sleep can adversely influence how individuals manage further interpersonal conflict. As discussed previously, poor sleep leads to diminished responses to emotional stimuli, and as a consequence, to the ability to manage stressful situations deteriorates.

Sleep is deeply embedded within the various processes that contribute to our everyday functioning. Therefore, a comprehensive understanding of the myriad ways in which sleep disturbances can interact with mental health difficulties is fundamental to the development of a meaningful, comprehensive formulation for the client.

KEY POINT

Sleep and mental health most likely interact in a bidirectional vicious cycle whereby mental health difficulties lead to loss of sleep, and loss of sleep subsequently contributes to even further incapacitated emotional regulation.

The role of sleep in psychological formulation

Short and Louca (2015) outlined the relevance of examining the link between insufficient sleep and mood deficits, as it highlighted the importance of preventative public health strategies targeting sleep and well-being. This begs the question as to whether implementing interventions to help normalise sleep disturbances within a clinical population has any effect on outcome of chronic mental health issues. Individuals who present with borderline personality traits or those experiencing acute anxiety or depression, coupled with experience of sleeping difficulties, are often at a significant risk for suicidal ideation (Pigeon et al. 2012). Sleep disturbances are reported to present as a greater risk factor for suicidal ideation than symptoms of depression or anxiety (Ribeiro et al. 2012). This has significant implications for suicide risk assessment, as sleep disturbances may be an important target for formulating an intervention plan. Selby (2013) suggested that targeting sleep disturbances in clinical populations may aid in improving their ability to manage stressful situations, employ coping skills and promote positive affect. A number of studies have reported favorable outcomes in using sleep-focused psychotherapy for individuals with depression (Lichstein et al. 2005; Harvey et al. 2011). PTSD or trauma-related sleep problems have been known to be resistant to first line treatments such as psychopharmacology or cognitive behavioural therapy for PTSD (Davidson et al. 2001; Zayfert and DeViva 2004). However, there is some evidence that behavioural interventions targeting sleep difficulties, in combination with first-line treatments can improve both daytime PTSD symptoms as well as sleep disturbance (Germain et al. 2007; Nakamura et al. 2011).

Integrating sleep into assessment and therapeutic dialogue

When generating questions pertaining to sleep, it is important to get a sense of the quality and quantity of sleep and how this affects daily living. It is also helpful to develop a timeline related to sleeping difficulties and the client's presenting problem to attempt to understand the degree to which they are related. The purpose of these questions is to gather as much information about:

1.   the nature and history of client's sleep patterns;
2.   current life stressors (including interpersonal difficulties, financial strain or occupational difficulties);
3.   environmental factors (such as a sleep hygiene, or the structure of the sleeping environment);
4.   the presence of any symptoms associated with a specific sleep disorder (including loud snoring, difficulty breathing, a tendency to fall asleep involuntarily, leg twitching);
5.   medical and psychiatric history (including medication use);
6.   current sleep habits (including if their occupation involves shift-work or frequent time zone travel, or whether they use substances known to interfere with sleep, such as caffeine, cigarettes, alcohol).

Morin (1993) suggested that directly asking about routines in relation to bedtime could elicit useful information in terms of a client's template for sleep. He also suggested that establishing the meaning that they attribute to quality of sleep, impact of sleep, and coping with sleep issues will give useful insights into the client's formulation of their own sleep difficulties.

KEY POINT

Information about sleep difficulties may not arise organically in assessment, as the client may view their sleeping problems as the least of their worries. The onus is on the practitioner to elicit such information through the use of open-ended questions.

Psychometric measures to assess sleep

It may be useful to use standardised measures to easily access data about a client's sleeping habits not covered in the clinical interview. The Sleep Quality Questionnaire (SQQ) (Kato 2014), is a measure that has been designed to examine sleep, well-being and quality of life as factors that are not mutually exclusive. Another, more established measure of sleep is the Pittsburgh Sleep Quality Index (PSQI), which is designed specifically for clinical populations and measures subjective sleep quality, sleep latency, duration, habitual sleep efficiency, sleep disturbances, use of sleeping medications and daytime dysfunction (Buysse et al. 1989). The validity and test-retest reliability of this measure has been established in a variety of studies (Buysse et al. 1991; Carpenter and Andrykowski 1998; Backhaus et al. 2002).

Conclusion

Sleep is a biological process that is essential for life and optimal health, both physical and mental. By incorporating information about sleep within a general formulation framework, practitioners can coherently link cognitive abilities, emotional intelligence, coping ability, insight and interpersonal behaviours. Given the complex bidirectional relationship described above between sleep and mental health, obtaining information on an individual's sleep quality and quantity during assessment could serve as a valuable tool in providing further information on an individual's patterns of cognition, emotional development, moods, patterns of behaviours and insight. Although sleep is not typically incorporated into psychological formulation, it is clear that merging it within a formulation framework could help generate a more comprehensive profile of psychological difficulties, as it can establish links between the other aspects of functioning. It could act as a mediating or moderating factor between precipitating and predisposing factors for distress. Understanding sleep profiles across the lifespan can assist with what might be maintaining a client's difficulties; as sleep and sleep disturbances often appear as a constant factor across a person's life. One of the greatest strengths and weaknesses of formulation is the flexibility afforded to the practitioner, whereby the understanding of distress can be constructed through different theoretical modalities. Harper and Spellman (2014) proposed that the boundaries surrounding the type of clinical information incorporated into formulation needed to be 'stretched' in order to cover the wide range of theoretical approaches, as well as the sheer level of individual difference in presentations. Having an understanding of quality of sleep and how it impacts on a person's wellbeing has clear implications for improving how mental health practitioners formulate psychological distress.

REFERENCES

Aigner, M., Graf, A.E., Freidl, M., Prause, W., Weiss, M., Kaup-Eder, B., Saletu, B. & Bach, M. 2003. Sleep disturbances in somatoform pain disorder. *Psychopathology*, 36(6), 324–328.

Anderson, C. & Platten, C.R. 2011. Sleep deprivation lowers inhibition and enhances impulsivity to negative stimuli. *Behavioural Brain Research*, 217(2), 463–466.

Assefa, S.Z., Diaz-Abad, M., Wickwire, E.M. & Scharf, S.M. 2015. The functions of sleep. *Neuroscience*, 2(3), 155–171.

Backhaus, J., Junghanns, K., Broocks, A., Riemann, D. & Hohagen, F. 2002. Test–retest reliability and validity of the Pittsburgh sleep quality index in primary insomnia. *Journal of Psychosomatic Research*, 53(3), 737–740.

Bailey, C.H. & Kandel, E.R. 2008. Synaptic remodeling, synaptic growth and the storage of long-term memory in aplysia. *Progress in Brain Research*, 169, 179–198.

Brown, S. & Völlm, B. 2013. Case formulation in personality disordered offenders: Views from the front line. *Criminal Behaviour and Mental Health*, 23(4), 263–273.

Buysse, D.J., Reynolds, C.F., Monk, T.H., Berman, S.R. & Kupfer, D.J. 1989. The pittsburgh sleep quality index: A new instrument for psychiatric practice and research. *Psychiatry Research*, 28(2), 193–213.

Buysse, D.J., Reynolds, C.F., Monk, T.H. & Hoch, C.C. 1991. Quantification of subjective sleep quality in healthy elderly men and women using the Pittsburgh Sleep Quality Index (PSQI). *Sleep: Journal of Sleep Research & Sleep Medicine*, 14(4), 331–338.

Carpenter, J.S. & Andrykowski, M.A. 1998. Psychometric evaluation of the pittsburgh sleep quality index. *Journal of Psychosomatic Research*, 45(1), 5–13.

Centers for Disease Control and Prevention 2016. 1 in 3 adults don't get enough sleep. Accessed online 24th July 2018 at https://www.cdc.gov/media/releases/2016/p0215-enough-sleep.html

Dallos, R. & Stedmon, J. 2014. Systemic formulation: Mapping the family dance, in Johnstone, L. and Dallos, R., eds., *Formulation in Psychology and Psychotherapy: Making Sense of People's Problems*. London: Routledge, 67–95.

Davidson, R., Rothbaum, B.O., van der Kolk, B.A., Sikes, C.R. & Farfel, G.M. 2001. Multicenter, double-blind comparison of sertraline and placebo in the treatment of posttraumatic stress disorder. *Archives of General Psychiatry*, 58, 485–492.

Diekelmann, S. & Born, J. 2010. The memory function of sleep. *Nature Reviews Neuroscience*, 11, 114–126.

Dudley, R. & Kuyken, W. 2014. Case formulation in cognitive behavioural therapy: A principle-driven approach, in Johnstone, L. and Dallos, R., eds., *Formulation in Psychology and Psychotherapy: Making Sense of People's Problems*. London: Routledge, 18–44.

Friedman, R.C., Bigger, J.T. & Kornfeld, D.S. 1971. The intern and sleep loss. *The New England journal of medicine*, 285(4), 201–203.

Geinisman, Y., Disterhoft, J.F., Gundersen, H.J.G., McEchron, M.D., Persina, I.S., Power, J.M., Van der Zee, E.A. & West, M.J. 2000. Remodeling of hippocampal synapses after hippocampus-dependent associative learning. *Journal of Comparative Neurology*, 417(1), 49–59.

Germain, A., Shear, M.K., Hall, M. & Buysse, D.J. 2007. Effects of a brief behavioral treatment for PTSD-related sleep disturbances: A pilot study. *Behaviour Research and Therapy*, 45(3), 627–632.

Gregory, A.M., Caspi, A., Eley, T.C., Moffitt, T.E., O'Connor, T.G. & Poulton, R. 2005. Prospective longitudinal associations between persistent sleep problems in childhood and anxiety and depression disorders in adulthood. *Journal of Abnormal Child Psychology*, 33(2), 157–163.

Gujar, N., Yoo, S.S., Hu, P. & Walker, M.P. 2011. Sleep deprivation amplifies reactivity of brain reward networks, biasing the appraisal of positive emotional experiences. *The Journal of Neuroscience*, 31(12), 4466–4474.

Harper, D. & Spellman, D. 2014. Formulation and narrative therapy: Telling a different story, in Johnstone, L. and Dallos, R., eds., *Formulation in Psychology and Psychotherapy: Making Sense of People's Problems*. London: Routledge, 96–120.

Harvey, A.G., Murray, G., Chandler, R.A. & Soehner, A. 2011. Sleep disturbance as transdiagnostic: Consideration of neurobiological mechanisms. *Clinical Psychology Review*, 31(2), 225–235.

Harvey, A.G., Talbot, L.S. & Gershon, A. 2009. Sleep disturbance in bipolar disorder across the lifespan. *Clinical Psychology: A Publication of the Division of Clinical Psychology of the American Psychological Association*, 16(2), 256–277.

Institute of Medicine, Committee on Sleep Medicine and Research, Board on Health Sciences Policy. 2006. *Sleep Disorders and Sleep Deprivation: An Unmet Public Health Problem*. Washington, DC: National Academies Press.

Jelicic, M., Bosma, H., Ponds, R.W.H.M., Van Boxtel, M.P.J., Houx, P.J., & Jolles, J. 2002. Subjective sleep problems in later life as predictors of cognitive decline. Report from the Maastricht Ageing Study (MAAS). *International Journal of Geriatric Psychiatry*, 17(1), 73–77.

Kato, T. 2014. Development of the sleep quality questionnaire in healthy adults. *Journal of Health Psychology*, 19(8), 977–986.

Killgore, W.D. 2010. Effects of sleep deprivation on cognition. *Progress in Brain Research*, 185, 105–129.

Killgore, W.D., Kahn-Greene, E.T., Lipizzi, E.L., Newman, R.A., Kamimori, G.H. & Balkin, T.J. 2008. Sleep deprivation reduces perceived emotional intelligence and constructive thinking skills. *Sleep Medicine*, 9(5), 517–526.

Lavie, P. 2001. Sleep disturbances in the wake of traumatic events. *New England Journal of Medicine*, 345(25), 1825–1832.

Leiper, R. 2014. Psychodynamic formulation: Looking beneath the surface, in Johnstone, L. and Dallos, R., eds., *Formulation in Psychology and Psychotherapy: Making Sense of People's Problems*. London: Routledge, 45–66.

Lichstein, K.L., Imau, S.D., McCrae, C.S. & Stone, K.C. 2005. Psychological and behavioral treatments for secondary insomnias, in Kryger, M.H., Roth, T. and Dement, W.C., eds., *Principles and Practices of Sleep Medicine*. Philadelphia, PA: W.B. Saunders.

Lim, J. & Dinges, D.F. 2010. A meta-analysis of the impact of short-term sleep deprivation on cognitive variables. *Psychological Bulletin*, 136(3), 375–389.

Maquet, P. 2001. The role of sleep in learning and memory. *Science*, 294, 1048–1052.

Meerlo, P., Havekes, R. & Steiger, A. 2015. Chronically restricted or disrupted sleep as a causal factor in the development of depression. *Current Topics in Behavioural Neurosciences*, 25, 459–481.

Morin, C.M. 1993. *Insomnia: Psychological Assessment and Management*. New York: Guilford Press.

Moro, L., Avdibegović, E. & Moro, I.N. 2012. Insight in psychotherapy. *Psychiatria Danubina*, 24(3), 46–47.

Nakamura, Y., Lipschitz, D.L., Landward, R., Kuhn, R. & West, G. 2011. Two sessions of sleep-focused mind–body bridging improve self-reported symptoms of sleep and PTSD in veterans: A pilot randomized controlled trial. *Journal of Psychosomatic Research*, 70(4), 335–345.

O'Brien, T. 2017. Feb 17 One-third of people get less than six hours a sleep a night. *The Irish Times*. Accessed online 24th July 2018.

Payne, J.D. & Kensinger, E.A. 2012. Sleep selectively benefits emotional aspects of scenes: Behavioral and neural evidence. *Psychophysiology*, 49, 11–15.

Payne, J.D. & Kensinger, E.A. 2018. Stress, sleep, and the selective consolidation of emotional memories. *Current Opinion in Behavioral Sciences*, 19, 36–43.

Phillips, A.J.K., Clerx, W.M., O'Brien, C.S., Sano, A., Barger, L.K., Picard, R.W., Lockley, S.W., Klerman, E.B. & Czeisler, C.A. 2017. Irregular sleep/wake patterns are associated with poorer academic performance and delayed circadian and sleep/wake timing. *Scientific Reports*, 7, 3216.

Pigeon, W.R., Britton, P.C., Ilgen, M.A., Chapman, B. & Conner, K.R. 2012. Sleep disturbance preceding suicide among veterans. *American Journal of Public Health*, 102(1), 693–697.

Poe, G.R., Walsh, C.M. & Bjorness, T.E. 2014. Cognitive neuroscience of sleep. *Progress in Brain Research*, 185, 1.

Ribeiro, J.D., Pease, J.L., Gutierrez, P.M., Silva, C., Bernert, R.A., Rudd, M.D., Joiner, T.E. 2012. Sleep problems outperform depression and hopelessness as cross-sectional and longitudinal predictors of suicidal ideation and behavior in young adults in the military. *Journal of Affective Disorders*, 3(136), 743–750.

Riemann, D. & Voderholzer, U. 2003. Primary insomnia: A risk factor to develop depression? *Journal of Affective Disorders*, 76(1), 255–259.

Ritsner, M., Kurs, R., Ponizovsky, A. & Hadjez, J. 2004. Perceived quality of life in schizophrenia: Relationships to sleep quality. *Quality of Life Research*, 13(4), 783–791.

Rosen, I.M., Gimotty, P.A., Shea, J.A. & Bellini, L.M. 2006. Evolution of sleep quantity, sleep deprivation, mood disturbances, empathy, and burnout among interns. *Academic Medicine*, 81(1), 82–85.

Ruhrmann, S., Schultze-Lutter, F., Salokangas, R.K.R., Heinimaa, M., Linszen, D., Dingemans, P., Birchwood, M. et al. 2010. Prediction of psychosis in adolescents and young adults at high risk: Results from the prospective European prediction of psychosis study. *Archives of General Psychiatry*, 67, 241–251.

Samkoff, J.S. & Jacques, C.H. 1991. A review of studies concerning effects of sleep deprivation and fatigue on residents performance. *Academic Medicine*, 66(11), 687–693.

Scott, J.P., McNaughton, L.R. & Polman, R.C. 2006. Effects of sleep deprivation and exercise on cognitive, motor performance and mood. *Physiology & Behavior*, 87(2), 396–408.

Selby, E.A. 2013. Chronic sleep disturbances and borderline personality disorder symptoms. *Journal of Consulting and Clinical Psychology*, 81(5), 941.

Short, M.A. & Louca, M. 2015. Sleep deprivation leads to mood deficits in healthy adolescents. *Sleep Medicine*, 16(8), 987–993.

Spoormaker, V.I. & Montgomery, P. 2008. Disturbed sleep in post-traumatic stress disorder: Secondary symptom or core feature? *Sleep Medicine Reviews*, 12(3), 169–184.

Staner, L., Luthringer, R. & Le Bon, O. 2006. Sleep disturbances in affective disorders, in Pandi-Perumal, S.R. and Monti, J.M., eds., *Clinical Pharmacology of Sleep*. Birkhäuser Basel, 101–124.

Steptoe, A., O'Donnell, K., Marmot, M. & Wardle, J. 2008. Positive affect, psychological well-being, and good sleep. *Journal of Psychosomatic Research*, 64(4), 409–415.

Sternberg, R.J. & Davidson, J.E., eds. 1996. *The Nature of Insight*. Cambridge, MA; London: The MIT Press.

Tempesta, D., Couyoumdjian, A., Curcio, G., Moroni, F., Marzano, C., De Gennaro, L. & Ferrara, M. 2010. Lack of sleep affects the evaluation of emotional stimuli. *Brain Research Bulletin*, 82, 104–108.

Tkachenko, O., Olson, E.A., Weber, M., Preer, L.A., Gogel, H. & Killgore, W.D. 2014. Sleep difficulties are associated with increased symptoms of psychopathology. *Experimental Brain Research*, 232(5), 1567–1574.

Van der Helm, E., Gujar, N. & Walker, M.P. 2010. Sleep deprivation impairs the accurate recognition of human emotions. *Sleep*, 33(3), 335–342.

Venkatraman, V., Chuah, L., Huettel, S. & Chee, M. 2007. Sleep deprivation elevates expectation of gains and attenuates response to losses following risky decisions. *Sleep*, 30(5).

Wagner, U., Gais, S., Haider, H., Verleger, R. & Born, J. 2004. Sleep inspires insight. *Nature*, 427(6972), 352–355.

Walker, M. 2017. *Why We Sleep: Unlocking the Power of Sleep and Dreams*. New York: Scribner.

Wilson, S. & Argyropoulos, S. 2012. Sleep in schizophrenia: Time for closer attention. *The British Journal of Psychiatry*, 200(4), 273–274.

Wong, M.M., Brower, K.J., Fitzgerald, H.E., & Zucker, R.A. 2004. Sleep problems in early childhood and early onset of alcohol and other drug use in adolescence. *Alcoholism, Clinical and Experimental Research*, 28(4), 578–587.

Zayfert, C. & DeViva, J.C. 2004. Residual insomnia following cognitive behavioral therapy for PTSD. *Journal of Traumatic Stress*, 17, 69–73.

Zohar, D., Tzischinsky, O., Epstein, R. & Lavie, P. 2005. The effects of sleep loss on medical residents emotional reactions to work events: A cognitive-energy model. *Journal of Sleep and Sleep Disorders Research*, 28, 47–54.

Chapter 7

Spirituality

Emma Breen, Julie Lynch, and Patrick Ryan

CHAPTER TOPICS

- Distinguishing between spirituality and religion
- Belief systems as both protective and risk factors for mental health
- Assessment of spiritual beliefs
- Integrating spirituality into formulation of psychological distress

Introduction

The purpose of formulation is to encapsulate a client's problems, to illustrate the relationship between various problems, to explain how difficulties may have developed from a psychological perspective and to guide psychological intervention (Johnstone and Dallos 2013). According to best practice, formulation is person-specific rather than problem-specific. Despite this, the focus of formulation and intervention has traditionally revolved around a client's difficulties, distress and disorders, ultimately neglecting the fundamental contribution of non-clinical information to the formulation process and lacking focus on the uniqueness of each person and their personal experience. This is not a new concept: '*It is much more important to know what sort of patient has a disease, than what sort of disease a patient has*' is an infamous maxim of Canadian-born physician William Osler (1849–1919). Despite this, practitioners have struggled to utilise the full range of information about a client generated from professional encounters, to the detriment of a comprehensive and meaningful formulation.

A client's experience of spirituality is one of many areas that tend to fall outside of the realm of 'clinically relevant information'. Practitioners seldom review and consider such information as part of the formulation process, despite the substantial impact that faith and belief systems can have an on individual's life and on the alleviation or maintenance of their psychological difficulties. It is reported that approximately 90% of the world's population engages in some form of religious or spiritual practice (Moreira-Almeida et al. 2014); therefore, practitioners (regardless of discipline or theoretical orientation) should be cognisant of the potential importance of spiritual or religious beliefs in relation to their client's presenting problems. An individual's experience of mental distress is inextricably intertwined with their sense of personhood and experience in the world, and while clinical symptomatology is undoubtedly part of their life experience, the meaning a person attaches to their experience of distress is even more likely to impact progress towards recovery. A sense of spirituality could be fundamental to this, and if so, can be validly utilised as part of the therapeutic process. The distinction between considering oneself as religious or as spiritual is an important one and is clarified in more detail in the following section. However, for the sake of simplicity and brevity for the remainder of the chapter, both will be referred to under the umbrella term of 'spirituality' unless otherwise stated.

This chapter encourages the practitioner to explore the potential utility of information on spirituality in developing a meaningful and useful formulation for their client. A comprehensive discussion of the literature in relation to spirituality and mental health will be presented. This sheds some light on the beneficial ways in which spiritual or religious beliefs can alleviate suffering, but also describes the maladaptive ways in which certain beliefs can contribute to the perpetuation of distress. The chapter reviews how the practitioner may incorporate the assessment of faith and belief systems into the clinical interview in a useful manner. Finally, examples of interventions which incorporate spirituality will be briefly highlighted to further emphasise the significance of merging both clinical and non-clinical information.

The meaning of spirituality

The adoption of a holistic approach in mental health care has stimulated the exploration of spirituality as one dimension of the cognitive, emotional, behavioural, interpersonal and psychological aspects that make up a human being. This has encouraged increased deliberation regarding the definition of spirituality, a complex multidimensional concept that has different meanings (Moreira-Almeida et al. 2014). Spirituality represents and symbolises different things to different people at different times in different cultures. However, the more common themes in the literature used to describe features of spirituality include:

1. A sense of purpose;
2. A sense of 'connectedness' (to self, others, nature, God or other);
3. A quest for wholeness;
4. A search for hope or harmony;
5. A belief in a higher being (or beings); and
6. Some level of transcendence, or the sense that there is more to life than the material or practical.

Underpinning many of these elements of spirituality is the assumption that we are intrinsically trying to make sense of the world around us and of our meaning and place within it. Accordingly, spirituality can be viewed as the mode through which meaning is sought, which varies depending on age, gender, culture, political ideology, physical or mental health amongst myriad other factors (Mental Health Foundation 2006).

Spiritual or religious?

Distinguishing between the words spiritual and religious is challenging because they have coinciding connotations, and yet are acknowledged to be distinct terms (Post and Wade 2009). Religion can be defined as a personal set or institutionalised system of religious attitudes, beliefs and practices. An active follower of a particular religion typically adheres to its rules, practices its rituals and associates (though not always) with other members of the same religion. Religion can be seen as the operational manifestation of an implicit, abstract and inherent set of beliefs about people, the world and the *what* and *why* of human existence. Spirituality is often viewed as a broader concept than religion as it is not limited to the confines of religious practice or overt behaviour. This then gives credence to some individuals identifying as 'spiritual but not religious'. Spirituality highlights qualities such as kindness, compassion, tolerance, service and community, and, in its truest sense, so does religion. However, where religion is defined by tradition and teachings, spirituality tends to be defined by what is real in each person's experience, and represents the search for a personally meaningful individual truth. That said, much of the empirical literature is dominated by a spirituality that is expressed through religion.

Spirituality and mental health

Clinical research on the relationship between spirituality and health (80% of which relates to mental health) finds that generally, the associations between spirituality and health are perceived as being positive. Spirituality is recognised as an important component of quality of life, and may be a critical resource for those coping with debilitating or terminal illnesses. However, there is a complex interplay between spirituality and mental health, and negative associations have been documented in the literature, for example, low spiritual well-being and religious struggle are associated with severe depression, hopelessness and a desire for hastened death. Such observations have encouraged clinicians and mental health practitioners to begin to assess and address spiritual concerns with their client in treatment and care.

Spirituality as a protective factor

Overall, research indicates that spirituality and religion are generally associated with greater well-being, enhanced coping resources and better mental health (Koenig 2012). Individuals who possess spiritual beliefs display less depression, anxiety, suicide attempts and experience enhanced quality of life, quicker remission of depressive symptoms and improved psychiatric outcomes (Moreira-Almeida et al. 2014). Spirituality is related to less depression in over 60% of 444 quantitative studies; improved well-being and happiness in almost 80% of 326 studies; enriched meaning and purpose in over 90% of 45 studies; and enhanced hope and optimism in over 75% of 72 studies (Koenig 2014).

Several mechanisms by which spiritual faith may exert positive effects on mental health have been discussed in the literature. Spiritual beliefs are often drawn upon to tolerate distress related to health problems, as well as to provide meaning for illness and stimulate hope for recovery. Spirituality or religion can contribute to positive mental health by connecting the individual to groups of like-minded people who can offer tangible and emotional support and encouragement (Levin 2009; Koenig 2014), as well as offering a sense of purpose in day-to-day life. Regular attendance at spiritual gatherings or engaging in a brief spiritual meditation each morning can offer an anchor around which other daily or weekly activities may be planned. Indeed, a recent study in the US has reported evidence that higher frequency of religious service attendance decreased the risk of depression in women (Li et al. 2016). Finally, spirituality may also promote rituals or behaviours that can orient one to the present moment to reduce anxiety (e.g. meditation and prayer). Spiritual behaviours such as meditative prayer can be helpful for emotional self-regulation, in that they may offer periods of modified awareness of cognitive processes and contribute to decreased worry or rumination processes that maintain emotional difficulties. This orientation to the present moment is often referred to as mindfulness. Mindfulness has long been linked to spirituality given that its roots are grounded firmly within Buddhist philosophy and tradition and its practices incorporate ways for purposefully paying attention to the present moment with an attitude of openness, nonjudgment and acceptance (Jacobs 2010).

Overall, enhanced coping resources for dealing with stress are likely to increase the occurrence of positive emotions and diminish the likelihood that stress will lead to emotional disorders such as anxiety, depression, suicide and substance abuse (Koenig 2012). Drawing upon one's spiritual beliefs can be a useful coping resource when faced with adversity, regardless as to whether the adversity represents difficult external environmental circumstances or internal vulnerability to mental difficulties.

Spirituality as a risk factor

Whilst most evidence suggests that spirituality provides meaning, optimism and comfort to the individual, a number of studies report associations between spirituality and negative outcomes (Allport and Ross 1967; Johnson et al. 2010). A 'spiritual struggle' (relevant only to the religious believer) has been reported to have a negative impact on mental health (Ellison and Lee 2010), and researchers in the US reported that belief in a punitive God is associated with psychiatric symptoms (Silton et al. 2014). Negative religious coping, although less prevalent (at least in the empirical literature), is linked with poorer quality of life (e.g. perceiving illness as a punishment from God) (Moreira-Almeida et al. 2014). Certain approaches to spirituality and religion may enhance feelings of guilt and shame by centring on wrong-doing or sin and subsequently could contribute to depression (Koenig 2012). Some religious individuals may pay more attention to their internal cognitive processes due to the assumption that thinking or acting in certain ways is sinful and is likely to be punished. Psychotic occurrences may have a religious orientation comprising delusions or distortions of normative religious beliefs. People with depression may experience ruminations regarding past wrongdoings resulting in a loss of connection with their higher power or may feel eternally damned (Baetz and Toews 2009).

An individual's struggles with the principles, practices, rituals and experiences linked to an organised religion are significant components to consider in the clinical context (Jacobs 2010). Research examining the impact of religious anti-gay prejudice on the mental health of the LGBTQ+ community is limited; however, recent evidence has suggested that greater exposure to prejudice associated with religious beliefs (e.g. that homosexuality is a sin) lends itself to higher levels of anxiety, stress and shame, as well problematic alcohol use for sexual minority groups (Sowe, Taylor and Brown 2017). Intrapersonal conflict between an individual's religious or spiritual beliefs and their sexual identity can result in attempted concealment of sexual orientation. A perceived lack of support within the individual's faith community can lead to alienation which perpetuates the anxiety, stress and shame. This prejudice may be experienced explicitly, such as physical or verbal abuse, or more implicitly, such as a lack of legal recognition of same-sex marriage.

Spirituality in mental health care

The concept of person-centred care represents a truly holistic approach to the individual suffering from mental turmoil and establishes a solid motive for integrating spirituality and religion into assessment, case formulation and therapy (Cox and Verhagen 2011). Aspects of an individual's spiritual or religious beliefs may be at the core of the client's distress (i.e. the presenting problem), or may represent a perpetuating or protective factor for the individual. A more developed understanding of the interplay between spirituality and mental health must be ascertained and careful exploration of spirituality and religion with clients must be encouraged amongst practitioners (Moreira-Almeida et al. 2014). Correspondence in the literature would suggest that at least some psychologists and psychiatrists do not consider it appropriate to encourage discussion of any spiritual or religious concerns with patients and thus neglect religious issues in clinical assessment (Kroll and Sheehan 1981; Neeleman and Lewis 1994). However, exploring clients' spirituality practices can undoubtedly facilitate both client's and clinician's comprehension of how meaning is made out of life crises, as well as how to improve ways of coping and living for the individual (Jacobs 2010). It is thus imperative that where appropriate, spirituality-related information is at least used to generate some hypotheses, and at best integrated into the construction of a formulation that will underpin psychological intervention.

Assessing spirituality

A wide range of behaviours, beliefs and emotions defines each faith group, and it is important to explore any relevant spiritual material to clarify its possible role in formulation. Establishing whether spiritual beliefs are a source of psychological distress, a protective factor or a coping resource is essential. This facilitates the identification of potentially helpful or unhelpful aspects of the client's beliefs and behaviours through differentiating between form and function. For example, the form of the behaviour 'helpful churchgoing' looks the same as 'unhelpful churchgoing' so, therefore, the issue does not revolve around the form but rather around the function it is perceived to have (Waller et al. 2010).

Assessing the spirituality and belief system of a client arguably requires a quantitatively different approach in mental health care, and a substantial literature base has been established regarding how practitioners might approach such sensitive issues in a respectful and constructive manner (Coyle and Lochner 2011). Moreira-Almeida and colleagues (2014) offer guidelines for completing spiritual assessment and subsequently incorporating this information into treatment. The purpose of taking a brief spiritual history includes learning about:

1. The individual's religious background;
2. The role spiritual/religious beliefs play in causing distress or coping with illness;
3. Beliefs that may influence or conflict with suggestions about care;
4. Participation in a spiritual community and whether this community is supportive; and
5. Any spiritual needs that might be unmet for the client.

Spirituality assessment can be conducted in a formal manner (such as using standardised questionnaires) or in an informal manner (e.g. through use of open-ended questions) (Post and Wade 2009). In the use of formal measures, experts in the field have reiterated the importance of utilising questionnaires that consist of items which are comprehensible and have consistent meaning, as ambiguity around the concept of spirituality can pose as an issue (Jager Meezenbroek et al. 2012). Monod and colleagues (2011) conducted a comprehensive systematic review to identify valid and reliable instruments used in clinical settings that measure spirituality, and concluded that the Functional Assessment of Chronic Illness Therapy – Spiritual Well-Being Scale (FACIT-Sp; Brady, Peterman, Fitchett, Mo and Cella 1999) and the Spirituality Index of Well-being (Daaleman, Frey, Wallace and Studenski 2002) were the most well-validated instruments for the formal assessment of a client's current spiritual state.

Obtaining information in an informal manner such as open-ended questions may be just as useful to the practitioner, as they allow for flexibility and adaptation based on the needs of each individual client. Several formats for informal spiritual history taking exist, including HOPE (Anandarajah and Hight 2001), FICA (Puchalski and Romer 2000), SPIRIT (Maugans 1996) and FAITH (Neely and Minford 2009). Across all aforementioned frameworks, spiritual resources, relationships, and other relevant information can be highlighted which may be significant for the assessment, conceptualisation and intervention phases of work with individuals. An outline of the FAITH framework for obtaining information on a client's spirituality is offered below.

FAITH framework for spiritual history-taking

The authors of FAITH (Neely and Minford 2009), a patient-centred framework for taking a spiritual history, originally proposed the mnemonic to aid medical professionals when taking a spiritual history from their patients. Comprehensive, holistic care is as important in mental health care as physical care; thus, this tool can be readily applied to the therapeutic setting. The FAITH framework is applicable and relevant for exploring both religious beliefs and also for clients whose spirituality lies outside the boundaries of traditional religious practice. A flexible set of questions is provided that can be adapted as required (See Table 7.1).

Assessment may occur during the initial stages of engagement or may arise organically following something the client says. For instance, Post and Wade (2009) highlight that if a client shares that they receive much support from their religious congregation then this may be followed up with questions regarding that support, their religious beliefs and how that has helped in the past. Through probing, further useful information about strengths and liabilities can be highlighted. During the initial assessment it is important to encompass questions regarding clients' spiritual/religious perspectives and experiences, particularly if their past or present spiritual/religious path is considered relevant for their presenting problems or as a source of potential resources for resolving difficulties (Coyle and Lochner 2011).

If spirituality or religion is an important part of a client's life, then asking general existential questions such as; 'What gives your life meaning?', 'What are your sources of comfort and strength when you are struggling with problems?', 'What helps you cope?' will highlight this. If the client is not spiritual or religious, then these questions may be useful in exploring and understanding their own personal world-view (Moreira-Almeida et al. 2014). In addition to the FAITH framework outlined above, areas that may warrant further consideration include:

- Type of religious coping and quality of relationship with a god or higher power (e.g. collaborative vs. passive).
- Moral concerns – this may raise questions regarding forgiveness.

Table 7.1 FAITH framework for spiritual history-taking

FAITH: Sample questions for taking a spiritual history

F   **Faith/spiritual beliefs**
    Do you have any particular faith, religious or spiritual beliefs?
    What gives your life meaning?
    What helps you cope in times of stress or illness?

A   **A**pplication
    In what ways do you apply your faith in your daily life?
    Do you belong to a particular church or community?
    Is prayer or meditation important to you?

I   **Influence/Importance of faith in life**
    How do your faith and spiritual beliefs influence your life? Are they important to you?
    How do your faith and spiritual beliefs influence you in this illness/distress? Have they
       altered your attitude or behaviour?
    Has this illness/distress influenced your faith?
    Do your beliefs influence or affect your healthcare decisions that would be helpful
       for me to know about?

T   **T**alk/**T**erminal events planning
    Do you have anyone you can trust to talk to about spiritual or religious issues?
    Do you have any specific requests if you were to become terminally ill? (N/A)

H   **Help**
    Is there any way I or another member of the health care team can help you?
    Do you require assistance or help with prayer?
    Would you like to speak to a chaplain?

• Possible sources of spiritual distress indicating negative religious coping. It is also important to distinguish when religious struggles are causes (e.g. too rigid/intolerant rules leading to inappropriate guilt) or consequences (e.g. excessive guilt in depression) of psychopathology.
• Spiritual/religious resources that may have been developed and used throughout their life that may be useful in coping with current problems.
• Spiritual experiences (near-death, out-of-body) may be life changing, but may increase fear and doubts since they may not align with the individual's previous worldview. Spiritual experiences may also resemble psychotic and dissociative disorders, requiring a differential diagnosis.
• Spiritual development: Previous positive and negative experiences regarding spirituality and religion that may have shaped the patient's current worldview.

In addition to benefiting the assessment, attaining a spiritual history may also suggest to clients that the clinician is considering the whole person, which may have positive implications for the therapeutic relationship (Moreira-Almeida 2014), and may also offer a useful challenge to how the distress has been explained up to the point of engaging in psychological services.

Integrating spirituality into clinical formulation and intervention

Research illustrates that spirituality influences various aspects of life, in particular mental health. Delivering care that addresses the whole person – body, mind and spirit is thus imperative (Koenig 2012). There are myriad ways in which the assessment and treatment of clients can be modified to incorporate spiritual dimensions. Campbell-Tunks (2014) reflected on one particular clinical case which encompassed viewing the bigger picture of the client's situation through a spiritual lens. In making this connection, the client was facilitated in embodying her valued spirituality in the context of family dynamics, which resulted in a meaningful change in relationships centred around increased openness, compassion, forgiveness and unconditional love (qualities which she strongly valued within her Christian faith). Another case study illustrated by Lea et al. (2015) highlighted how an individual's religious community and religious interpretations impacted the development and maintenance of an eating disorder. The eating disorder originated to an extent out of struggles with perfectionistic tendencies aligned with religious beliefs that had been misunderstood and misapplied. Spiritual pathways to recovery were utilised as part of the intervention; for example, one pathway focused on *mindfulness and spiritual mindedness*, which helped to challenge incorrect thoughts and negative, self-judgmental feelings and encouraged the individual to connect with mind, body and heart/feelings in order to feel connected to herself, to feel connected to God and to feel connected to others.

Ramos et al. (2014) demonstrated how the client's spirituality can be incorporated into therapeutic skill sets. For example, if an individual's beliefs are more closely linked to peaceful imagery than to prayer, then incorporating more spiritually focused visual skills such as guided and vivid imagery would be more beneficial. The thought-stopping skill could integrate a visual stop sign and a redirection of attention to deep breathing corresponding with the image of a flowing river and the statement 'Life is like a river you have to navigate....let yourself be carried because you can't control everything' (Ramos et al. 2014, p. 273). By integrating the client's spirituality into therapy when appropriate, the influence of the active ingredients of therapy may be augmented, such as the therapeutic alliance and the satisfaction with therapy received (James and Wells 2003). Some further ways in which spirituality can be integrated into formulation and intervention are discussed below.

Cognitive behavioural model

Cognitive-behavioural theorists propose that beliefs and thoughts underlie human affect and behaviour. In particular, core beliefs affect perceptions and produce automatic thoughts in response to specific situations that result in emotional states (Beck 1995). Theorists have emphasised the significance of core beliefs about oneself, the world and the future in relation to emotions and for some individuals such beliefs may incorporate spiritual themes (Rosmarin et al. 2011). Such core spiritual beliefs can greatly influence one's perception of self and others. For example, an Irish Catholic woman who has had an abortion in the past and has never told anyone may experience overwhelming shame as her core spiritual beliefs revolve around morality, abortion as a sin and a subsequent perception of herself as a 'bad person'. It is important to be aware of how this information and the meaning made of the situation fits into an understanding of her presenting problem.

Researchers have examined the cognitive-behavioural mechanisms which may explain the association between spirituality and mental health. James and Wells (2003) suggested that religious beliefs (schema) offer a mental model for managing the appraisal of life events and are vital in self-regulation of thinking processes. They propose that religious attributions for life events may result in a sense of meaning, perceived control and predictability especially during times of high stress. The sense of meaning may aid reframing challenges as a spiritual opportunity, a wake-up call or even punishment. Religious behaviours that reduce self-focus and worry are positively associated with mental health as they contribute to self-regulation whilst providing a calming effect (e.g. contemplative prayer and mindfulness meditation). In contrast, religious behaviours that increase self-focus and worry are linked with intrusive thoughts, poor thought control and mental illness (Baetz and Toews 2009).

Further illustrating this point, Rosmarin et al. (2011) explored how spiritual core beliefs may be included in a cognitive model of worry. Trust in god may support positive spiritual emotions, religious coping and a sense of connectedness with transcendence, which may promote increasing tolerance for uncertain life situations. Mistrust in god may amplify intolerance of uncertainty by encouraging fundamental questions, doubts, conflicts and struggles with the Divine throughout stressful periods of life. Rosmarin and colleagues illustrated that maladaptive negative beliefs linked to mistrust in god were effectively targeted, which resulted in decreased symptoms of anxiety, demonstrating a framework in which spiritual beliefs can be integrated into cognitive theory.

Mindfulness as a spiritual practice

In the so-called third wave of empirically based psychological orientations, mindfulness was introduced as a therapeutic practice by John Kabat-Zinn with mindfulness-based stress reduction (MBSR) and has subsequently become fundamental to three other therapies: Mindfulness-Based Cognitive Therapy (MBCT), Dialectical Behaviour Therapy (DBT), and Acceptance and Commitment Therapy (ACT). These approaches are well-established and widely used in mental health care and may represent a truly fundamental component of intervention for the spiritual client.

Spirituality in overcoming addiction

It has been suggested that spirituality and religion are particularly relevant to recovery in addictive behaviour. Individuals engaged with Alcoholics Anonymous (AA) describe recovery as a 'spiritual awakening' (Delaney et al. 2009). Spirituality may aid with recovery from addiction, as addiction has been linked with feelings of meaningless existence. Developing spirituality can therefore be a protective factor and a positive resource that can be drawn upon instead of filling a 'meaningless' void. Spiritual practices are a core feature of substance abuse programs with specific practices such as surrender, confession, giving and seeking forgiveness, prayer and meditation. These practices may enhance spiritual health, and clients may be less inclined to relapse into substance abuse (Delaney et al. 2009).

Conclusion

Current practice based evidence indicates that practitioners should work to understand their clients' meaning-making systems where information on spirituality can be routinely integrated, where appropriate, into formulation and intervention. A strong sense of spiritual identity may have a positive effect on mental health by providing meaning for physical and mental distress, stimulating hope for recovery and aiding in emotional self-regulation by way of regular meditative prayer. On the other hand, religious or spiritual beliefs may contribute to emotional distress for those who believe in a punitive god or those whose religion is not tolerant of diverse sexual orientations. Religious prejudice against the LGBTQ+ community can be explicit, such as physical or verbal abuse, or implicit, that is, lack of legal recognition of same-sex marriage. Each spiritual faith group carries a wide range of behaviours, beliefs and emotions; therefore, it is imperative to explore relevant spiritual material with the client to clarify its possible role in formulation. Formal standardised measures for spirituality assessment are available, as well as several formats for informal spiritual history taking (i.e. the FAITH framework). Interventions for psychological distress can be modified to incorporate spiritual dimensions in myriad ways, including the introduction of mindfulness as a spiritual practice, and integrating spiritual beliefs into CBT-based work.

Reflective exercise

Consider the case of Joe, a 62-year-old man who presented to your service with low mood and suicidal ideation. In your holistic approach to assessment, you included some open-ended questions to gather a brief spiritual history. You learned that Joe had always considered himself a devout Catholic and regularly attended mass in his local church until his wife passed away from cancer last year. Joe considered the death of his wife to be a punishment from God and has since isolated himself from church and his spiritual community. Reflect on the following questions in relation to Joe's case.

- How might Joe's religious beliefs be influencing his current presentation?
- In what ways might Joe's beliefs be maintaining his distress?

- How could his faith act as a protective factor?
- Speculate on the kind of formulation that may have been constructed for Joe had you not acquired any information about his spirituality. How useful do you think that formulation would be to Joe's situation? Note the difference in approach that might be taken, in light of the information on his reported beliefs and behaviours.

REFERENCES

Allport, G.W., & Ross, J.M. 1967. Personal religious orientation and prejudice. *Journal of Personality and Social Psychology*, 5(4), 432–443.

Anandarajah, G., & Hight, E. 2001. Spirituality and medical practice: Using the HOPE questions as a practical tool for spiritual assessment. *American Family Physician*, 63(1), 81–89.

Baetz, M., & Toews, J. 2009. Clinical implications of research on religion, spirituality, and mental health. *La Revue Canadienne de Psychiatrie*, 54(5), 292–301.

Beck, J.S. 1995. *Cognitive Therapy: Basics and Beyond.* New York: The Guildford Press.

Brady, M.J., Peterman, A.H., Fitchett, G., Mo, M., & Cella, D. 1999. A case for including spirituality in quality of life measurement in oncology. *Psycho-oncology*, 8, 417–428.

Campbell-Tunks, D. 2014. The empowerment of translating spirituality into practical living. *Spirituality in Clinical Practice*, 1(4), 293–296.

Cox, J., & Verhagen, P.J. 2011. Spirituality, religion and psychopathology: Towards an integrative psychiatry. *The International Journal of Person Centred Medicine*, 1(1), 146–148.

Coyle, A., & Lochner, J. 2011. Religion, spirituality and therapeutic practice. *Psychologist*, 24(4), 264–266.

Daaleman, T.P., Frey, B.B., Wallace, D., & Studenski, S. 2002. The spirituality index of well-being: Development and testing of a new measure. *Journal of Family Practice*, 51(11), 952.

Delaney, H.D., Forcehimes, A.A., Campbell, W.P., & Smith, B.W. 2009. Integrating spirituality into alcohol treatment. *Journal of Clinical Psychology*, 65(2), 185–198.

Ellison, C.G., & Lee, J. 2010. Spiritual struggles and psychological distress: Is there a dark side of religion? *Social Indicators Research*, 98(3), 501–517.

Jacobs, C. 2010. Exploring religion and spirituality in clinical practice. *Smith College Studies in Social Work*, (80), 98–120.

Jager Meezenbroek, E., Garssen, B., Van den Berg, M., Van Dierendonck, D., Visser, A., & Schaufeli, W.B. 2012. Measuring spirituality as a universal human experience: A review of spirituality questionnaires. *Journal of Religion and Health*, 51(2), 336–354.

James, A., & Wells A. 2003. Religion and mental health: Towards a cognitive-behavioural framework. *British Journal of Health Psychology*, 8(3), 359–376.

Johnson, M.K., Rowatt, W.C., & LaBouff, J. 2010. Priming Christian religious concepts increases racial prejudice. *Social Psychological and Personality Science*, 1(2), 119–126.

Johnstone, L., & Dallos, R. (Eds.) 2013. *Formulation in Psychology and Psychotherapy: Making Sense of People's Problems.* London, New York: Routledge.

Koenig, H.G. 2012. Religion, spirituality, and health: The research and clinical implications. *International Scholarly Research Network*, 1–33.

Koenig, H.G. 2014. The spiritual care team: Enabling the practice of whole person medicine. *Religions*, 5(4), 1161–1174.

Kroll, J., & Sheehan, W. 1981. Religious beliefs and practice among 52 psychiatric inpatients in Minnesota. *American Journal of Psychiatry*, 146, 67–72.

Lea, T., Scott Richards, P., Sanders, P.W., McBride, J.A., & Kawika Allen, G.E. 2015. Spiritual pathways to healing and recovery: An intensive single-N Study of an eating disorder patient. *Spirituality in Clinical Practice*, 2(3), 191–201.

Levin, J. 2009. How faith heals: A theoretical model. *Explore (NY)*, 5, 77–96.

Li, S., Okereke, Ol., Chang, S.C., Kawachi, I., & VanderWeele, T.J. 2016. Religious service attendance and lower depression among women – A Prospective Cohort Study. *Annals of Behavioural Medicine*, 50(6), 876–884.

Maugans, T.A. 1996. The SPIRITual history. *Archives of Family Medicine*, 5, 11–16.

Mental Health Foundation 2006. The Impact of Spirituality on Mental Health: A Review of the Literature. Available at: http://www.mentalhealth.org.uk/content/assets/PDF/publications/impact-spirituality.pdf?view=Standard (Accessed 14 October 2015).

Monod, S., Brennan, M., Rochat, E., Martin, E., Rochat, S., & Bula, C.J. 2011. Instruments measuring spirituality in clinical research: A systematic review. *Journal of General International Medicine*, 26(11), 1345–1357.

Moreira-Almeida, A., Koenig, H.G., & Lucchetti, G. 2014. Clinical implications of spirituality to mental health: Review of evidence and practical guidelines. *Revista Brasileira de Psiquiatria*, 36(2), 176–182.

Neeleman J., & Lewis G. 1994. Religious identity and comfort beliefs in three groups of psychiatric patients and a group of medical controls. *International Journal of Social Psychiatry*, 40, 124–34.

Neely, D., & Minford, E. 2009. FAITH: Spiritual history-taking made easy. *The Clinical Teacher*, 6, 181–185.

Post, B.C., & Wade, N.G. 2009. Religion and spirituality in psychotherapy: A practice-friendly review of research. *Journal of Clinical Psychology*, 65(2), 131–146.

Puchalski, C., & Romer, A.L. 2000. Taking a spiritual history allows clinicians to understand patients more fully. *Journal of Palliative Medicine*, 3(1), 129–137.

Ramos, K., Barrera, T.L., & Stanley, M.A. 2014. Incorporating nonmainstream spirituality into CBT for anxiety: A case study. *Spirituality in Clinical Practice*, 1(4), 269–277.

Rosmarin, D.H., Pirutinsky, S., Auerbach, R.P., Björgvinsson, T., Bigda-Peyton, J., Andersson, G., Pargament, K.I., & Krumrei, E.J. 2011. Incorporating spiritual beliefs into a cognitive model of worry. *Journal of Clinical Psychology*, 67(7), 691–700.

Silton, N.R., Flannelly, K.J., Galek, K., & Ellison, C.G. 2014. Beliefs about God and mental health among American adults. *Journal of Religion and Health*, 53(5), 1285–1296.

Sowe, B.J., Taylor, A.J., & Brown, J. 2017. Religious anti-gay prejudice as a predictor of mental health, abuse and substance use. *American Journal of Orthopsychiatry*, 87(6), 690–703.

Waller, R., Trepka, C., Collerton, D., & Hawkins, J. 2010. Addressing spirituality in CBT. *The Cognitive Behaviour Therapist*, 3(3), 95–106.

Chapter 8

Sexuality

Patrick Ryan, Marie Kennedy, and Julie Lynch

CHAPTER TOPICS

- Sexual identity, orientation and behaviour and their relationship to mental health
- Relevance of practitioner factors when discussing sexuality
- Sensitive and respectful assessment of sexuality

Introduction

Sexual experiences, personalised or shared, are an integral part of the human experience. Each society and culture, however, interprets sexuality, its expression and manifestation in different ways at different times in unique fashions. Norms, morals and values of each society dictate what is considered to be acceptable sexual activity (Boundless 2015). While the topic of sex and sexuality may no longer be the biggest taboo for clients attending psychological services in Western culture, it remains a profound but delicate force to be reckoned with in professional encounters. This is especially obvious when it starts to become dysfunctional, or when its absence in someone's life becomes the source of frustration, depression, anxiety or anger (Diamond 2014). The vast amount of information obtained in a clinical intake interview makes it difficult to decipher relevant versus irrelevant information for any formulation process, particularly when some of the information (such as the sexual life of a client) may not necessarily align with traditional conceptual frameworks. Despite this, non-clinical information can be very useful (and sometimes fundamental) in understanding a client's distress. How a client experiences and manages their 'sexual being' can contribute to the formulation of a client's problem including in predisposing factors (e.g. sexual abuse can impact a person's future sexual experience); precipitating factors (e.g. a negative experience of 'coming out' about one's sexuality); maintaining factors (impotence could maintain low mood); protective factors (a satisfying intimate relationship) or even the problem behaviour itself (e.g. sexual identity disorder).

On occasion, or more often in specialist services, a client may explicitly state that a sexual difficulty is their main reason for attending a service. When this occurs, the sexual difficulty has priority and the interview takes on a direction that can include direct lines of enquiry and the use of formal assessment measures. This chapter, however, reflects on generating information about a client's sexual world that is not offered explicitly. To begin with, the evolution of the concept of sexuality in humankind will be explored. Following this, sexuality will be discussed in relation to three separate but interconnected dimensions: Sexual orientation, sexual identity and sexual behaviour. Given the silence that often surrounds this particular component of the human experience, the practitioner's approach in eliciting information about the client's sexual self will require careful and mindful application that enhances the therapeutic relationship. Examples for therapeutic dialogue that may capture the nature of such information are considered. In addition, available measures to generate a more comprehensive profile of the client will be outlined. Finally, the chapter will conclude with how typical sexual and clinical information can be merged to understand distress in a more comprehensive manner, along with suggested directions for future research.

KEY POINT

The sexual life of a client may offer fundamental contributions to the understanding and formulation of a client's distress as potential predisposing, perpetuating or problem factors.

Evolving definition of sexuality over time

The last 50 years have witnessed an explosion of literature on sexuality, which has resulted in the development of sexuality theory. Despite this and the increased attention on sexuality in our culture, defining sexuality remains ambiguous. While sexual behaviour is as old as humankind, sexuality, as a concept, was not introduced into language until recent centuries. The term first appeared in the 1800s, specifically relating to sex as a reproductive function (Heath 1982). In 1889, the word was used by a physician to describe the surgical removal of a woman's ovaries to refer to the human capacity for sexual feelings. Since then it has been used repeatedly, both in medical and other settings, and its meaning has becoming more and more complex. In the nineteenth century, the sciences of psychology and sexology began to emerge, which began to classify, describe and quantify human sexual behaviour. In 1994, Laumann, Gagnon and Michaels suggested a model that helped to understand human sexuality. This model described human sexual experience in terms of attraction, behaviour and identity, which may or may not be constant. This idea was framed by Ollis et al. (2001) in a model called the sexual trichotomy. This model postulates that identity (how we identify as male, female or transgender), sexual orientation (who we are attracted to) and sexual behaviour (or sexual acts) are fluid and have the capacity to change over time. This and other iterations of the concept have encouraged flexibility around thinking about sexuality as a more multi-dimensional concept than simply heterosexuality and homosexuality or indeed, gender.

Sexual gender or identity

Identity refers to one's sense of self, thus the term gender identity refers to one's sense of self as male, female or transgender (APA 2011). Sex is assigned at birth and is determined primarily by physical attributes such as the internal and external anatomy of the newborn. Gender on the other hand, refers to socially constructed roles and behaviours that society considers appropriate for boys and girls. When one's gender identity and biological sex are not matching, the individual may identify as transsexual or another transgender category (cf. Gainor 2000). An increasing body of research has documented an association between difficulties in managing sexual identity and orientation with mental health difficulties.

Sexual orientation

Sexual orientation refers to the gender of those to whom one is romantically and sexually attracted. Categories of sexual orientation generally include attraction to members of the other gender (heterosexuals), attraction to members of one's own gender (gay men or lesbians) and attraction to members of both genders (bisexuals). While these categories are still widely used, research has proposed that sexual orientation does not necessarily appear in such definite categories and instead perhaps it occurs on a continuum (e.g. Kinsey, Pomeroy, Martin and Gebhard 1953; Klein 1993). This open discussion and expression of gender identity and orientation in the media highlights society's growing interest and openness to variance in how the sexual self is both experienced internally and expressed externally. While sexual orientation and identity is becoming less binary, a significant number of people still experience distress associated with their sexual identity and orientation, which in many cases can contribute to initiating or maintaining psychological distress.

KEY POINT

The practitioner should endeavour to use inclusive language and terminology that does not make assumptions about a client's orientation or behaviour.

Lesbian, Gay, Bi-sexual and Transgender (LGBT) people may have a higher risk of mental health difficulties (Mayer et al. 2008). This is often in response to societal and cultural expectations pertaining to perceived norms about identity, roles and behaviour. This premise suggests that how a person experiences their sexual orientation, internally and externally, could predispose them to mental health difficulties. Gay people in Ireland are seven times more likely to attempt suicide than heterosexual people, with the disapproval of family members a contributing factor to this elevated risk (Cannon 2013). The Psychological Society of Ireland (PSI) has published Guidelines for Good Practice with Lesbian, Gay and Bisexual Clients that provide specific information about the distinctive experiences of LGBT people (PSI 2015). Experiences of homophobia and the process of 'coming out' are two examples of significant distress experienced by LGBT people. Of course, how tolerant the environment is, is critically important. The higher the level of prejudice and intolerance, the more difficult it is to discuss sexual orientation, often leading to a spiral of self-silencing. This underlines the need for practitioners to be aware of complexities in the process of coming out (i.e. It is more than saying 'I am x or y...') and highlights where they can play a positive role for those who seek help with this process (Moane 2015). As coming out can be a very difficult process for some people (potentially a precipitating factor to mental health difficulties), an opportunity to discuss their sexuality in a safe space will not only support self-efficacy, but also offer the unique opportunity to develop a purposeful sense of connection to their own narrative. Given this, the practitioner needs to be especially mindful that sexual orientation may have a significant part to play in a given presenting problem, but its communication may well be tentative or presented in an opaque manner.

Sexual behaviour

Sexual functioning is an important component for quality of life and for sustaining a satisfying intimate relationship (Zemishlany and Weizman 2008); it may even act as a protective factor against stress for some individuals. Sexual dysfunction can affect one's perception of self-value and self-esteem and can impair the sense of security in sexual relationships (Raja and Azzoni 2003). Sexual dysfunction is a common issue in the general population, affecting approximately 23% of men and 32% of women in Europe (Nicolosi et al. 2006). While much of modern society remains uncomfortable talking freely about sexual behaviour, the Diagnostic and Statistical Manual of Mental Disorder, Fifth Edition (DSM-5; American Psychiatric Association 2013) acts as a reminder of what can go wrong for people. Sexual dysfunction as described in the manual includes disorders of desire, arousal, penetration and orgasm. These diagnoses of sexual dysfunction are almost certainly influenced by and influence other illnesses commonly treated by practitioners. Sexual dysfunctions could present as the problem behaviour, predispose or precipitate a mental health difficulty, or maintain a problem (e.g. impotence may exacerbate and perpetuate low mood; Perelman 2011).

Sexual dysfunction is a complex presentation often experienced by people who have untreated mental health difficulties, or as an adverse effect of psychiatric medications. Approximately 20%–43% of people treated with second-generation psychotropic treatments and 36%–56% of people taking newer psychiatric medications experience some form of sexual dysfunction (Bobes et al. 2003).

If a person's sexual behaviour is affected by their medication, this can contribute to feelings of low self-esteem and low mood. For instance, a common source of situational anorgasmia (inability to orgasm) is the use of anti-depressants, including selective serotonin reuptake inhibitors (SSRIs). Although reporting of anorgasmia as a result of SSRIs is not exact, studies suggest 17%–41% of users of such medications are affected by a form of sexual dysfunction (Landén et al. 2005). In these cases, the stress-vulnerability-coping model proposes that sexual dysfunction as a result of medication is considered a high stress factor (precipitating factor) that increases the burden of illness, negatively affects client's adherence to their treatment (maintaining factor) and can contribute to relapse or deterioration of mental health (Stimmel and Gutierrez 2006).

Even without the use of medication, reports of sexual dysfunction and frustration with their sex life are common amongst people with long-term mental health difficulties (Raja and Azzoni 2003). Sexual dysfunction can often be a first sign of, and co-exist with psychological ill health. For example, a reduction in sexual desire may be a presenting problem for some clients, who after direct enquiry are found to have symptoms of low mood and depression. For other individuals, reduction in sexual desire may precede the start of a depressive episode (Schreiner-Engel and Schiavi 1986). Knowledge of the prevalence and presentation of sexual dysfunctions in clients would improve the attitude of the treating practitioner towards sexual difficulties and possibly result in increased compliance with treatment for the client (Zemishlany and Weizman 2008). For clients on medication, an awareness of their general perception of their own sexual narrative will contribute to the formulation by directly allowing for assessment of any potential relationship between their medication and their sexual lives (Phelps et al. 2015). To provide comprehensive care for our clients, practitioners must be knowledgeable of the relationship between mental and sexual health because despite the high incidence of sexual dysfunction, clients rarely report sexual difficulties to their practitioners voluntarily (Moreira et al. 2005).

KEY POINT

An understanding of the relationship between mental and sexual well-being is fundamental to providing comprehensive care to clients.

Practitioner factors

Gathering information pertinent to the sexual aspects of a client's developmental history has the potential to enhance, enrich and deepen the formulation process. The approach of the mental health practitioner plays a pivotal role in the successful collation of this information. Factors such as demonstrating comfort with the topic, initiating the dialogue around the client's particular and unique sexual narrative, appropriate use of humour and normalising the client's distress are addressed below.

Confidence initiating conversation

In order to gather data on a client's sexual self, the practitioner must open avenues for exploration normally by asking clear and unambiguous questions. Unfortunately, however, this does not always happen. Approximately 74% of health care providers rely on their clients to initiate a discussion about their sexual health (Association of Reproductive Health Professionals and the National Women's Health Resource Centre 2009). A large-scale online survey reported that 40% of female participants did not talk to their practitioner about a sexual health difficulty, although half of them wanted to (Berman et al. 2003). Apprehension around initiating such discussions is likely to be multi-faceted. A lack of training and skills to deal with these specific concerns is regularly reported, as well as embarrassment and discomfort in talking about sex. Practitioners tend to underestimate the frequency of sexual dysfunction among their clients and the impact these difficulties have on their client's overall well-being. Concern about offending clients, assumptions that people experiencing mental health problems lack interest in sexual activity and poor understanding of the physical and psychological effects of medications on sexuality are all cited as reasons as to why practitioners may side-step a discussion about sexual health (Higgins, Barker and Begley 2005). Whatever the reason, there remains a significant discrepancy between the kind of information and care clients need regarding their sexual health and what they are being offered (Kingsberg 2006).

KEY POINT

Practitioner factors such as comfort, confidence, appropriate use of humour and normalising statements are pivotal to eliciting information on clients' sexuality while maintaining rapport and enhancing the therapeutic relationship.

Building rapport

Successful interviewing begins with building a strong rapport. While this is naturally integral to the development of the therapeutic relationship in general, it is particularly crucial that, prior to a discussion around sexual well-being, clients are at ease and have developed trust, confidence and comfort with the practitioner. However, the principles of developing useful working relationships pertain: the practitioner should adopt a professional atmosphere and demeanour along with starting out with clinic policies, informed consent, the limits of confidentiality and release of information policies at the beginning of the interview. The practitioner should then give an opportunity for clarity and questions before they advance to the next step (Hersen and Thomas 2007). Religious views and socio-cultural factors can influence people's willingness to discuss sexual health issues with health professionals (Peitl et al. 2009), but exploring such issues openly and explicitly will help to diffuse unhelpful assumptions, as well as setting up learning experiences for both client and professional.

Demonstrating comfort and using humour appropriately

It has been reported that clients feel more comfortable when the practitioner demonstrates comfort with the topic (Sadovsky and Nusbaum 2006; Parish and Kingsberg 2011). Practitioners should use simple, direct language and if possible, they should model the level of explicitness of the sexuality discussion, whilst remaining in their comfort zone. Sexuality issues should be discussed as openly as other issues, with maintained eye contact and a steady demeanour. Clients will take their cues from the practitioner, who should set a serious tone, but one that may be loosened if the client demonstrates receptiveness to humour. Humour may be helpful in increasing a client's comfort with the topic; however, the humour should only reference the interviewing situation or the issue itself, never the client (Hersen and Thomas 2007). Humour can help diffuse difficult situations or can be a way of avoiding a difficult-to-name situation – the art of the therapeutic encounter is to know where, when, how and if to introduce it. If it has therapeutic value, it is worth considering; if it does not, it may be better to refrain from using it. The use of language is important and requires careful consideration. Technical language offers the benefit of 'professional objectivity' but can leave clients at a loss as to meaning; colloquial language can have nuanced, unintended meaning that can cause confusion in the communication. An agreement and commitment to checking in on what is being communicated, not communicated or miscommunicated can help to address this whilst also offering opportunities for mutual learning (and occasionally, humour).

KEY POINT

Gentle humour, when used in a compassionate, considerate way, can diffuse difficult conversations and increase a client's comfort with the topic.

Normalising the issue

Normalising statements can help to put the client at ease and allow them to see their situation in context. If issues in sexual narrative are hinted at or explicitly emerge, normalising the issue and emotional response, along with reframing attention to the related problem are a legitimate priority. Clients can be hesitant about seeking help for issues in their sexual lives; therefore, the practitioner should offer reassurance that it is difficult to talk about sexual well-being and any relationship difficulties that may result (LoPiccolo 2004). The use of open-ended questions to stimulate curiosity and discussion is recommended to expand on emerging difficulties. In particular, directive open-ended questions can focus the topic whilst avoiding a prescribed response. Note that 'how' questions rather than 'why' questions can help with opening exploration and minimising the need to justify or defend. Other crucial features of the practitioner's approach include an awareness of the client's culture, guaranteeing confidentiality (or its limits), and avoidance of judgement, ageism and assumptions about sexual identity, orientation and monogamy (Sadovsky and Nusbaum 2006).

Assessing sexual lives

While the initial interviews are key to eliciting both clinical and non-clinical information relating to the client's distress, standardised measures can sometimes serve as a useful platform upon which to build a discussion around sensitive issues between the practitioner and client. Such measures can also safely provide a platform for follow-up questions that may be necessary to gather a more comprehensive profile of the client's experience. There are two main types of measures at the practitioner's disposal to generate discussion around sexuality. The first is the use of generic intake measures that include some aspect of sexual health and well-being; the second is the use of specific measures of sexuality questionnaires.

Generic measures that include items on sexuality

A broad based measure that may create opportunity to open discussion on issues related to the sexual self is the Beck Depression Inventory – II (BDI-II) (Beck, Steer and Brown 1996). The BDI-II is a widely used 21-item self-report inventory measuring the severity of depression in adults. This screening measure while designed to assess levels of depression, includes a question pertinent to the sexual health, regarding loss of libido. The four-point response scale ranges from 'I have not noticed any recent change in my interest in sex' to 'I have lost interest in sex completely'. This simple question could be sufficient to gently initiate a conversation about issues related to the client's sexual well-being and at least displays an openness to this type of conversation as a typical part of the assessment process.

Specific measures that assess sexual identity, orientation and behaviour

If a client volunteers sexuality issues as the primary concern for attending a service, there are more specific measures that can offer practitioners a quick, reliable method of gathering data about their client's sexuality and sexual functioning. For example, Epsteins' Sexual Orientation Inventory (ESOI) (Epstein 2006) is a measure that allows the individual to determine where they are on the sexual orientation continuum. Sexual dysfunction can be assessed through measures that (i) identify and diagnose sexual dysfunction; (ii) measure the severity of a sexual problem; (iii) determine the effectiveness of a treatment and detect change in symptoms; (iv) measure the individual's satisfaction with the intervention; (v) assess the impact of a dysfunction upon an individual's wellbeing; and (vi) understand the impact of the dysfunction on the partner and relationship (Giraldi et al. 2011). Sample sexual dysfunction questionnaires include the following: The Sexual Dependency Inventory (Carnes and Delmonico 1994), The Internet Sex Screening Test (ISST; Delmonico 1997) and Decreased Sexual Desire Screener (DSDS) (Clayton et al. 2009). It is important to note that measures of sexual function often exclude important domains and lack applicability to gender and sexual orientation. In a study by Arrington and colleagues (2004), questionnaires measuring sexual function were identified, the domains most commonly assessed were determined and the evidence for their usefulness was examined. Out of 62 questionnaires identified, only nine demonstrated both adequate reliability and validity. Therefore, measures should truly only be considered as an adjunct to the clinical interview (Arrington et al. 2004).

Open-ended questioning during the clinical interview

While items from various standardised measures can stimulate follow-up questions that may elicit relevant information about the client's sexual world, open-ended questions during professional encounters can be equally lucrative. It is recommended that the practitioner use inclusive terms and language that do not make assumptions about a client's sexual identity, orientation or behaviour, particularly in cases where such information is not openly volunteered. Sample questions that make assumptions about a client's sexuality can include 'Are you married or single?' or asking a female client 'Do you have a partner?' Rather, the practitioner should ask inclusive questions such as 'Are you currently in a relationship?' or 'What is your level of commitment to your partner?' These statements and the deliberate use of inclusive language convey to the client that the practitioner is open to hearing about his or her sexual identity, orientation and functioning. The following is a series of further questions that may also be helpful in enhancing the therapeutic dialogue. The interviewer should follow up responses with open-ended or clarifying questions.

- How may your sexual development or history relate to your current distress?
- What is your experience of intimate relationships? What was that like for you?
- How do you understand your sexual orientation or preferences?
- Has your sexuality ever caused you any difficulties? If so, can you tell me a bit more about that?
- How would you describe your sexual development across your life?
- Describe any sexual experiences where you did not feel comfortable with what was happening.

KEY POINT

The use of language in discussing sexuality is crucially important and requires careful consideration on the practitioner's behalf.

Conclusion

Sexual well-being and functioning are core components of the human experience, and have an important role to play in clinical formulation due to their relationship with both mental health and mental distress. The limited number of useful objective assessment measures for sexual issues makes effective interviewing crucial. While meaningful and purposeful clinical interviewing is a valid method of assessment for all mental distress, it is vital in generating useful information about the sexual lives of clients. Clients will appreciate the willingness of the practitioner to broach issues related to sexual development, well-being and functioning if that is seen as offering further insights into their general psychological health, and so explaining this link is an important educational task during the assessment and formulation process. Reliable and valid measures that include questions pertaining to sexual well-being may offer a safe way of collecting relevant information. Additionally, if the client is experiencing specific sexual difficulties, there are psychological measures that can be effectively used to assist with assessment of such difficulties. Although measures of sexuality can be simple to use and efficient, they should not be used as a substitute for engaging in comprehensive history taking that emerges from safe, professional relationship encounters. Creating and maintaining a dialogue space to discuss sexual issues, feeling heard and discussing interventions, all enrich the relationship between the client and practitioner (Althof and Parish 2013) and ultimately leads to enriched data that can be used in formulation of the presenting psychological distress.

Reflective exercise

Take some time to work through the following reflective exercise on the development of your own perceptions regarding sexual identity, orientation and behaviour. They may relate to your spiritual faith, your core beliefs or your own personal experiences. As practitioners, if we fail to deconstruct the norms, values and perceptions about sexual well-being that we have acquired from our own particular upbringing, we risk carrying these perceptions into the therapeutic space with us allowing them to dictate how the therapeutic dialogue is generated.

- Reflect on your personal opinion about the following:
  - Equal marriage rights regardless of gender
  - Having more than one partner

- Teenage pregnancy
- Sexually explicit media (i.e. pornography)
- What constitutes a relationship
- Sexual orientation as a continuum
- Which of these (if any) evoke particularly strong feelings for you?
- How do you make sense of these responses?
- How might your perceptions on the above affect how likely you are to broach such a topic with your client?

REFERENCES

Althof, S. E. & Parish, S. J. 2013. Clinical interviewing techniques and sexuality questionnaires for male and female cancer clients. *The Journal of Sexual Medicine*, 10, 35–42. [online] Available doi: 10.1111/jsm.12035 [Accessed 20 Sep 2015].

American Psychological Association 2011. The Guidelines for Psychological Practice with Lesbian, Gay, and Bisexual Clients, adopted by the APA Council of Representatives, February 18–20, Available on the APA website at http://www.apa.org/pi/lgbt/resources/guidelines.aspx

American Psychiatric Association 2013. *Diagnostic and Statistical Manual of Mental Disorders*, 5th ed. Arlington, VA: American Psychiatric Publishing.

Arrington, R., Cofrancesco, J. & Wu, A. W. 2004. Questionnaires to measure sexual quality of life. *Quality of Life Research*, 13(10), 1643–1658. Springer.

Association of Reproductive Health Professionals and the National Women's Health Resource Centre (now Healthy Women) 2009. Women's Sexual Health: Provider Survey. [online] Available at: www.arhp.org/Publications-and-Resources/StudiesandSurveys/SHY-Survey [Accessed 6 Sep 2015].

Beck, A. T., Steer, R. A. & Brown, G. K. 1996. *Manual for the Beck Depression Inventory-II*. San Antonio, TX: Psychological Corporation.

Berman, L., Berman, J., Felder, S. et al. 2003. Seeking help for sexual function complaints. What gynaecologists need to know about the female client's experience. *Fertility and Sterility*, 79, 572–576.

Bobes, J., A-Portilla, M., Rejas, J., Ndez, G., Garcia-Garcia, M. & Rico-Villademoros, F. 2003. Frequency of sexual dysfunction and other reproductive side-effects in clients with schizophrenia treated with risperidone, olanzapine, quetiapine, or haloperidol: The results of the EIRE study. *Journal of Sex & Marital Therapy*, 29(2), 125–147.

Boundless 2015. 'Human Sexuality and Culture' Boundless Psychology, Available at https://www.boundless.com/psychology/textbooks/boundlesspsychology-textbook/genderand-sexuality-15/sexuality-415/human-sexuality-and-culture-299-12834/ [Accessed 21 Aug 2015].

Cannon, M. 2013. Gay people in Ireland seven times more likely to attempt suicide. *The Sunday Times*, Irish edition [online], 31 March 2013, available: http://seanduke.com/2013/04/01/gay-people-in-ireland-seven-times-more-likely-to attempt-suicide/- [accessed 21 Aug 2015].

Carnes, P.J. & Delmonico, D.L. 1994. *Sexual Dependency Inventory*. Wickenburg, AZ: The Meadows Institute.

Clayton, A. H., Goldfischer, E. R., Goldstein, I. S. et al. 2009. Validation of the decreased sexual desire screener (DSDS): A brief diagnostic instrument targeted for generalized acquired female hypoactive sexual desire disorder (HSDD). *Journal of Sexual Medicine*, 6(3), 730–8.

Delmonico, D. L. 1997. Internet Sex Screening Test. [Online] Available at: http://www.sexhelp.com

Diamond, S. 2014. Why sex is still such a central concern in psychotherapy. *Psychology Today* [online], 10 May 2014 available: https://www.psychologytoday.com/blog/evildeeds/201405/the-psychology-sexuality [accessed 21 Aug 2015].

Epstein, R. 2006. Do gays have a choice? *Scientific American Mind*, 50–57.

Gainor, K. A. 2000. Including transgender issues in lesbian, gay, and bisexual psychology: Implications for clinical practice and training. In: B. Greene & G. L. Croom (Eds.), *Psychological Perspectives on Lesbian and Gay Issues: Vol. 5. Education, Research, and Practice in Lesbian, Gay, Bisexual, and Transgendered Psychology: A Resource Manual*, 131-160.

Giraldi, A., Rellini, A., Pfaus, J., Bitzer, J., Laan, E., Jannini, E. A. & Fugl-Meyer, A. R. 2011. Questionnaires for assessment of female sexual dysfunction: A review and proposal for a standardized screener. *Journal of Sexual Medicine*, 8, 2681–706.

Heath, S. 1982. *The Sexual Fix*. London: Macmillan Press.

Hersen, M. & Thomas, J. C. 2007. *Handbook of Clinical Interviewing with Adults*. SAGE Publications.

Higgins, A., Barker P. & Begley, C. 2005. Neuroleptic medication and sexuality: The forgotten aspect of education and care. *Journal of Psychiatric and Mental Health Nursing*, 12(4), 439–446.

Kingsberg, S. A. 2006. Taking a sexual history. *Obstetrics and Gynecology Clinics North America*, 33, 535–547.

Kinsey, A. C., Pomeroy, W. B., Martin, C. E. & Gebhard, P. H. 1953. *Sexual Behaviour in the Human Female*. Philadelphia, PA: W.B. Saunders.

Klein, F. 1993. *The Bisexual Option*. New York: The Harrington Park Press.

Landén, M., Högberg, P. & Thase, M. E. 2005. Incidence of sexual side effects in refractory depression during treatment with citalopram or paroxetine. *The Journal of Clinical Psychiatry*, 66(1), 100–6.

LoPiccolo, J. 2004. Sexual Disorders Affecting Men. In: L. J. Haas (Ed.), *Handbook of Primary Care Psychology*, 485–494. New York: Oxford University Press.

Mayer, K. H., Bradford, J. B., Makadon, H. J., Stall, R., Goldhammer, H. & Landers, S. 2008. Sexual and gender minority health: What we know and what needs to be done. *American Journal of Public Health*, 98, 989–995. 10.2105/AJPH.2007.127811.

Moane, G. 2015. Psychology along the spectrum of human sexuality. *The Irish Times* [online], 14 Jul 2015, available: http://www.irishtimes.com/life-and-style/health-family/psychology-along-the-spectrum-of-human-sexuality-1.2275416 [Accessed 30 Aug 2015].

Moreira, J. E., Brock, G., Glasser, D., Nicolosi, A., Laumann, E. & Paik, A. 2005. Help seeking behaviour for sexual problems: The Global Study of Sexual Attitudes and Behaviors. *International Journal of Clinical Practice*, 59(1), 6–16.

Nicolosi, A., Laumann, E., Glasser, D., Brock, G., King, R. & Gingell, C. 2006. Sexual activity, sexual disorders and associated help-seeking behavior among mature adults in five anglophone countries from the Global Servey of Sexual Attitudes and Behaviors (GSSAB). *Journal of Sex & Marital Therapy*, 32(4), 331–342.

Ollis, D. et al. 2001. *The Sexual Trichotomy Model, in Catching On: Teaching and Learning Activities*. Victoria: Department of Education, Employsment and Training.

Parish, S. J., & Kingsberg, S. 2011. The sexual health interview: Female. In: J. P. Mulhall, I. Goldstein & R. C. Rosen (Eds.), *Cancer and Sexual Health*. New York: Human Press; 291–305.

Peitl, M., Peitl, V. & Pavlovic, E. 2009. Influence of religion on sexual self-perception and sexual satisfaction in clients suffering from schizophrenia and depression. *International Journal of Psychiatry in Medicine*, 39(2), 155–167.

Perelman, M. A. 2011. Erectile dysfunction and depression: Screening and treatment. *Journal of Clinical Urology, North America*, 38(2), 125–39.

Phelps, K. W., Jones, A. B. & Payne, R. A. 2015. The interplay between mental and sexual health. In: N. Gambescia, G. R. Weeks and K. M. Hertlein (Eds.), *Systemic Sex Therapy*, 2nd ed. Taylor & Francis Group.

Psychological Society of Ireland (PSI) 2015. *Guidelines for Good Practice with Lesbian, Gay and Bisexual Clients*. Health Service Executive.

Raja, M. & Azzoni, A. 2003. Sexual behavior and sexual problems among clients with severe chronic psychoses. *European Psychiatry*, 18(2), 70–6. PubMed.

Sadovsky, R. & Nusbaum, M. 2006. Sexual health inquiry and support is a primary care priority. *The Journal of Sexual Medicine*, 3, 3–11.

Schreiner-Engel P. & Schiavi R.C. 1986. Lifetime psychopathology in individuals with low sexual desire. *Journal of Nervous Mental Disorders*, 174, 646–51.

Stimmel, G. L. & Gutierrez, M. A. 2006. Counselling clients about sexual issues. *Pharmacotherapy*, 26(11), 1608–15.

Zemishlany, Z. & Weizman, A. 2008. The impact of mental illness on sexual dysfunction. In: R. Balon (Ed.), *Sexual Dysfunction. Advances in Psychosomatic Medicine*, Med 29, 89–106.

Chapter 9

Physical activity

Dermot McMahon and Patrick Ryan

CHAPTER TOPICS

- The role of the Elaboration Likelihood Model in the implementation of sport and exercise into clinical formulation
- A review of evidence supporting the psychological benefits of engaging in sport and exercise
- Positive psychology and the integration of personalised science
- Inclusion of the DICE-PM model and questions relating to sport and exercise for inclusion in balanced clinical interview assessment

Introduction

The chapter explores the process by which clinicians reach helpful assertions regarding the presenting difficulties of a person. More specifically, how a dynamic understanding is derived from interview data or dialogue is explored. Central to this critique is consideration of the level of clinical relevance assigned to particular types of interview data. Physical activity, through the particular lens of sport and exercise, is used as a working example of an area of a person's life likely to be considered low in clinical relevance. Arguments for the potential clinical relevance of all contextual data derived at interview are presented before recommendations for application to practice, and an introduction to supportive theoretical models, are made. Addressing the potential relevance of sport and exercise in case formulation provides an exemplar frame for application of these recommendations. Suggested interview questions to support inclusion of additional contextual variables in assessment and formulation of a person's presenting difficulties are presented for consideration at the conclusion of the chapter.

The assessment and formulation process

Criteria for clinical psychology education programmes outline that clinical psychologists should utilise a formulation process which uses professional and research skills in work with clients based on a scientist-practitioner and reflective-practitioner model. This model should incorporate a cycle of assessment, formulation, intervention and evaluation (Health Professions Council, 2009; British Psychological Society, 2017).

The British Psychological Society Best Practice Guidelines (2017) sets out formulation as:

> ...the summation and integration of the knowledge that is acquired by the assessment process
>
> (British Psychological Society, 2017)

Johnstone acknowledges the complex nature of the task of 'formulation'. She encourages clinical psychologists to draw on broad-based skills in their development of a dynamic understanding of a client's difficulties. The BPS Division of Clinical Psychology 2001 (cited in Johnstone and Dallos 2006) assert formulation to be a process. It defines formulation as:

> The summation and integration of the knowledge that is acquired by the assessment process (which may involve a number of different procedures). This will draw on psychological theory and data to provide a framework for describing a problem, how it developed and is being maintained.
>
> (Johnstone and Dallos, 2006, p. 4).

Johnstone and Dallos (2013) provide a comprehensive overview of how clinicians make sense of people's problems and note the limited quantity of research within the psychological formulation field at that time. Although interest in the processes by which clinicians reach the understanding of a person that informs decisions about their care has advanced, empirical research has continued to focus on established frameworks for drawing together and making sense of client data. There appears to be a relatively small volume of research attempting to open new directions to the process. Definitions of the 'sense making' process of formulation remain open to interpretation. The latter definition cited here refers to a 'number of different (potential) procedures' (Division of Clinical Psychology 2001). This perhaps invites an attitude of curiosity and creativity in its application. It seems fair to assert that the psychological assessment and formulation process can be treated as that – a fluid process incorporating data collection, synthesis and analysis.

It seems appropriate to define what is commonly referred to as 'data' by way of introduction to consideration of the process of psychological assessment and formulation. 'Data' tends to refer to any and all information about a person gathered through a variety of methods of assessment and considered clinically relevant. Clinical relevance could be defined as the level of significance assigned to particular types of data as represented by their common inclusion or exclusion from an accepted understanding of the person, and their particular set of presenting difficulties. Patterns are evident in the types of information commonly considered relevant to the development of understanding that ultimately informs intervention tailored to the individual.

Many mental health practitioners, and specifically clinical psychologists, endorse a biopsychosocial appraisal of a client's presenting difficulties (Carr & McNulty, 2011). Adoption of this broad-based model of understanding facilitates development of a dynamic understanding of a person's presenting difficulty in terms of the biological, psychological and social factors that may predispose the person to greater likelihood of experiencing psychological distress. It is likely that adoption of this perspective has inspired common questions posed at clinical interview, questions that encourage disclosure of particular types of data. This data (information) generally centres on the person's developmental and family history, current functioning and beliefs regarding the presenting difficulty. Many services providing psychological assessment and intervention tend to develop a standardised assessment protocol targeting specific information deemed clinically relevant in line with this particular perspective.

Psychological difficulties appear to be most commonly considered in the context of predisposition, reported events precipitating onset and factors that may either maintain their presence, or protect the person from the detrimental effects of the difficulty. These elements are asserted by prominent authors (i.e. Carr & McNulty, 2011) to be the core components of the perspective adopted by many mental health practitioners in their approach to client difficulties.

KEY POINT

The formulation approach, which takes into account predisposing, presenting, precipitating, perpetuating and protective factors influenced by the biopsychosocial model is well placed to integrate sports and exercise into the decision-making process.

Psychological assessment and formulation: A critical perspective

Established methods of psychological assessment hold value in terms of their evidence-supported nature. However, progress with regard to the integration or attempted unification of approaches appears limited. Methods of assessment vary between and within professional health disciplines. For example, at the within-discipline level; clinical psychologists will vary in terms of emphasis on specific types of data depending on the individual psychologist's allegiance to a particular theoretical model or combination of models. Clinicians conducting an assessment with an individual and working within a cognitive-behavioural frame may attend most to specific behaviours performed in response to certain stimuli. The same clinician working with that client within a primarily psychodynamic frame may focus more heavily on apparent maladaptive ways of relating and the potential influence of their own biases as a therapist on the understanding being developed. Carr and McNulty (2011) outline international efforts to unify assessment across the psychiatry discipline. Perhaps any perceived lack of unification of approach, between or within disciplines, may only inspire creativity in therapeutic work with people with mental health difficulties.

This chapter aims to highlight how physical activity through sport and exercise can usefully add to the formulation process. Brewer et al. (2011) asserts the power of peripheral message cues on clinicians' judgement relating to clients' psychological status. Brewer et al. draw on the 'Elaboration Likelihood Model' of social persuasion (Petty and Cacioppo, 1981, cited in Brewer et al. 2011) in his consideration of expert judgement formation. This model is proposed to explain the action between analytic and systemic cognitive processing of information deemed relevant or central to the message topic (i.e. presenting difficulty in case formulation) and peripheral or irrelevant information (i.e. heuristics).

Brewer et al. (2011) provide empirically sound support for the asserted prevalence of inferences derived from cognitive short-cuts, such as 'heuristic processing' in clinician judgement regarding clients' need for treatment, illness severity and distress. Drawing on previous consideration here of the application of a biopsychosocial model as frame of reference for psychological assessment and formulation, any data (client information) not deemed directly relevant to 'sense making' within that frame may be likely considered peripheral. The work of Brewer et al. inspires important questions about the influence of clinician impressions, their foundations and the importance of reflective practice and acknowledgement of personal biases on the part of the practitioner. Brewer and colleagues advocate for a clinician's reflexive practice, a deliberate exploration of their own cognitive processing style and appropriate use of this awareness in client work.

KEY POINT

Clinicians engaging in the formulation process may benefit from reflexive practice during sense making: The Elaboration Likelihood Model offers an insight into the importance of clinicians self-recognising personal biases and countertransference which may affect clinician impressions of client presentation during a psychological assessment, for example, suitability for referral to sports and exercise.

Sport and exercise

"Sport has long been recognised for its ability to bring people together, to act as a face for inclusion, to foster relationships and to enhance the reputation of Ireland both here and overseas. Sport is something that can impact on all of Ireland's people."

(Federation of Irish Sport, 2014, p. 8).

The Irish Sports Council (ISC) conducts large-scale biannual research providing insight into sports participation levels and key population group differences in Ireland. This publication supports informed development of national guidelines regarding issues pertaining to physical activity in Ireland (Irish Sports Monitor, 2013). The ISC reports a recent upsurge in participation in individual sporting activities including running, cycling, weights training, dancing, swimming and triathlon. Areas of reported positive change include: A closing gender gap in participation levels with female participation levels appearing to be accelerating and increased meeting of recommended levels of physical activity across most population subgroups. However, under representation of those of lower socioeconomic status, those with disabilities and young males are highlighted as concerns (Irish Sports Monitor, 2013). It is worth highlighting that these groups are also those widely recognised to be at increased risk of mental health difficulty.

"Sport has a positive impact on the lives of those who take part. It is not just health benefits that sport can deliver but also social lives and people's sense of belonging and even educational and professional attainment".

(Federation of Irish Sport, 2014, p. 9).

In 2014, the Federation of Irish Sport (FIS) asserted that Ireland was on course to be the country with the fattest citizens in Europe by 2025. Of note is the lack of specific reference to mental health across recent sports and exercise related government publications. Publications appear to emphasise the reported physical health benefits related to participation in sport and exercise and the positive impact participation is asserted to have on tourism and other sources of national revenue. The indirect impact of participation on the Irish population's mental health (and indeed the economic impact of this) appears largely unrecognised. The report cites statistics claiming that 84% of highly active people report being in a good mood most of the time compared to 75% of those who are sedentary (FIS, 2014).

Sheard (2013) cites the work of pioneering sports psychology scientist practitioners (Griffith, 1926; Tutko et al. 1969) who examined the personality profiles of superior athletes. These studies (conducted 43 years apart) reported strikingly similar findings. They listed courage, determination, emotional control, trust, optimism and buoyancy as some of the commonly held characteristics of successful athletes. Sheard (2013) considers the construct 'mental toughness' at length.

Clients seeking psychological services are often vulnerable by definition; they are in need of special care. An understanding of 'mental toughness' and its relationship to sports participation could offer clinicians an additional lens in their analysis of client data. Perhaps if a client demonstrates unmet needs with regard to sports and exercise, for example, expresses interest but reports difficulty accessing resources, then these observations could inform intervention supporting increased 'mental toughness'. Inherently, this may indirectly support development of some of the characteristics above counteracting vulnerability. This hypothesis is likely to prove over-simplistic, and a more dynamic perspective is required to generate assessment data to support a meaningful formulation.

KEY POINT

Sheard's psychological profile of successful athletes offers a potential framework for evaluating the integration of sports and physical activity in formulation and potential benefits of building resilience. Multidisciplinary collaboration is also key to ensure clinical recommendations are maintained and put into practice when appropriate for the client.

Weinberg and Gould (2011) provide an extensive overview of the psychological variables commonly associated with increased sport and exercise participation. They refer to the intra- and inter-personal dynamics at play in sport. Sport is asserted to be central to socialisation, particularly for young men. Spending time with friends and family is shown to be the primary motivator for women aged over 25 to participate in sport and exercise (FIS, 2014). A review by Kern (2016) concludes that physical activity is associated with greater quality of life and less psychological distress in both clinical and nonclinical populations. Kern suggests that exercise may be a viable intervention option for some mental health difficulties. She notes methodological shortcomings of the research cited but reports effects comparable to psychotherapy and psychoactive medication.

A balanced view of the potential impact of participation or nonparticipation in sports and exercise should consider the unique experience of the individual. Factors that facilitate a sense of 'belonging' for one person may maintain a sense of alienation for another. Humans vary in their interests, and the impact of individual level differences in interest or participation in sport may be underestimated.

KEY POINT

There is strong evidence linking sports and exercise participation with improved self-reported quality of life, mental health and physical health outcomes among respondents. However, a person-centred model of care must ensure vulnerable clients are provided with recommendations that match their personal motivation and treatment aims.

Anecdotal evidence from practitioners often highlights the potential for individuals to identify themselves as 'different' when their primary interests do not match those of their peers. The psychological literature relating to sports tends to centre on participation, achievement, competition and mental 'toughness' (see Weinberg and Gould 2011; Sheard 2013). Holding a view congruent with this may cause distress if the client is unable to engage with behaviour that reflects this value system. Similarly holding a view that opposes this value system would also cause distress (a sense of being different). Consideration of the position held by an individual in terms of the importance of sport and exercise in their life may provide insight for clinicians to understand the core beliefs the individual holds regarding self and others, as well as how they experience belonging and social connectedness. This understanding may form an important part of a developing understanding of the presenting difficulty under consideration.

Drawing on Bronfenbrenner's Ecological Systems theory (1979), sports and exercise related beliefs may impact a person at multiple levels. At the macro-system level the individual is likely to be impacted by cultural expectations, perhaps as indicated by the type of language used in national policy pertaining to the topic area (i.e. sport and exercise as per the working example here). Messages regarding the importance of participation in sports, in terms of positive associations with socialisation and educational and professional attainment may foster a set of expectations in an individual. Again, these expectations are likely to include both the positive action of the relationship—participate and succeed—and its opposite action.

Narratives pertaining to the importance of participation (and doing well) in sport and exercise may also impact an individual at the micro and exo-systemic levels. Bronfenbrenner asserted these levels to include family and neighbourhood/environmental influences respectively. Level of concordance within immediate family members, with regard to interest and participation in sport, may foster a sense of union or division within families. At the exo-systemic level, an individual may identify as part of an 'in' or 'out' group among peers depending on sharing or non-sharing of interests.

Consideration of the unique experience of sport and exercise for the individual could inspire new foci for therapeutic dialogue and indeed additional specific questions during professional encounters. A brief list of questions inspired by the current discussion is included in the closing section of this submission. These suggested questions may complement traditional models of psychological assessment and formulation construction by encouraging dialogue with a new focus. On the other hand, a balanced consideration of a client's difficulty within their own unique context will go beyond dominant ideas of sport and exercise participation as solely a strength or resource. The practitioner may find themselves asking at what point one person's primary protective factor becomes a maintaining factor of difficulty for another. For example, positive appraisals of participation in sport and exercise alone could prove unhelpful with some client groups, such as those with eating disorders and/or who are addicted to exercise. It is becoming more apparent how inclusion of an area considered low in clinical relevance may bring depth to the assessment and formulation process.

KEY POINT

Clinicians may draw on Bronfenbrenner's Ecological Systems theory during the assessment process to explore how cultural and social factors can impact the integration of sport and exercise into clients' recovery plans: The social integration afforded by sport may be directly beneficial for clients seeking a stronger social network.

Synthesis of clinical and non-clinical data

Quantitative assessment data

Comprehensive psychological assessment usually requires implementation of both standardised and other modes of data collection. Thus far, issues pertaining to data collection through interview have been considered. An outline of available standardised measures with relevance to sport and exercise participation with demonstrated validity will complement discussion of issues pertaining to clinical interview.

Tenenbaum, Eklund and Kamata, 2012 suggest that both extrinsic and intrinsic motivation in sport related activity can be measured using the following instruments that account for context and situation:

1. Context Measures – Exercise Motivation Scale (EMS; LI 1999); Behavioural Regulation in Exercise Questionnaire (BREQ; Mullan, Markland, & Ingledew,1997); Sport Motivation Scale (SMS; Pelletier et al., 1995); Sport Motivation Scale-6 (SMS-6; Mallet, Kawabata, Newcombe et al., 2007); Pictorial Motivation Scale (PMS; Reid, Vallerand, Poulin & Crocker, 2009).
2. Situational Measures – Situational Motivation Scale (SIMS; Guay, Valleran, & Blanchard, 2000).

For example, the Sport Motivation Scale (SMS) (Pelletier et al. 1995, cited in Tenenbaum et al. 2012) is a well established measure with demonstrated validity and reliability consists of seven subscales that measure three types of Intrinsic Motivation (IM) and three forms of extrinsic motivation. The 'Amotivation' subscale measures phenomena whereby individuals experience feelings of incompetence and lack of control (Deci and Ryan, 1985). Inclusion of a measure of intrinsic and extrinsic motivation for sports and exercise could prove complementary to traditionally used measures of psychological well-being and distress with clinical populations. Use in conjunction with, for example, the Beck Depression Inventory (Beck 1961) could aid development of a dynamic understanding of the affective and physical/somatic experience of a person reporting low mood. Inferences about potentially difficulty-maintaining cognitions may be further contextualised, with an indication of an individual's motivational style and participation in sport and exercise.

Qualitative assessment data

There appears to be a movement among practitioners who prefer to work from empirical evidence bases towards a quest for dynamic models of assessment that can be realistically applied in the real world setting of the clinical encounter. Opening up assessment to a broad perspective of the person's life may, in time, lead to better understanding of the dynamic interplay of *all* factors influencing the person. However, this is an inherently complex and ambitious task. Restricting a focus to information deemed clinically relevant to the specific 'problem' is likely to limit exploration in assessment. The type of top-down (analytical & systematic) derivation of inferences commonly conducted by experts (Brewer et al. 2011) fails to acknowledge the dynamic nature of both the difficulties under consideration and the context of the individual themselves. Level of participation in sport and exercise is likely to represent only one small part of that context.

Fisher (2015) describes the dynamic nature of the causes and effects of psychological distress. He highlights a contradiction in the development of diagnostic criteria listed in the Diagnostic and Statistical Manual of Mental Disorders, 5th Edition (DSM-V) (American Psychological Association, 2013). The DSM-V is commonly adopted as a frame of reference for assessing distress and disorder. Diagnostic label categories within the DSM are usually derived via calculation of inferential statistics, that is, they are derived at group, and not individual, level. Therefore, it could be suggested that expert clinical judgement is potentially confounded in a layered manner. The expert clinician's perception of the client's context (and difficulty) is likely to be influenced by both:

1. Central-message (i.e. diagnostic criteria) cues impacting on what peripheral information is attended to (as explained by the Elaboration Likelihood Model in the study of heuristics previously outlined; Petty and Cacioppo 1981); and
2. Undetermined moment-to-moment predictive effects of symptoms on one another.

However, there is a lack of acknowledgment of the complex interplay of biological, psychological, social and emotional systems within individuals when approaching assessment from this top-down perspective. Fisher (2015) proposes a general frame and method for dynamic assessment. He outlines a framework for an approach that first identifies all relevant sources of data for the diagnostic system. He asserts that data should then be collected with as much detail as possible before consideration of the relative contribution of each to the presenting difficulty. Finally, he asserts that a comprehensive understanding of the dynamic interrelationship between each factor would strengthen the validity of resulting inferences (and recommendations for personalised care). Perhaps the suggestions posed in the current discussion, with regard to collection of quantitative and qualitative data relating to sport and exercise participation, would aid inclusion of this facet of a person's life in dynamic assessment.

This discussion has thus far centred on the premise that all client information holds potential clinical relevance and that ideal assessment methods would tap all potentially useful data. Perhaps not enough credit is given to existing methods of data collection and integration. Eells et al. (2011) present evidence relating to expert reasoning processes among psychotherapists. They cite literature supporting the status of formulation as centrally important in evidence-based practice. They assert that 'better' formulations are those that demonstrate comprehensiveness, elaboration and following of a systematic process. Furthermore, expert formulations were defined by greater descriptive, diagnostic, inferential, and treatment planning information. Expert formulations prioritised given and inferred symptoms, adult relationship history, inferred psychological mechanisms, the ongoing need for further evaluation, and on plans to focus on treatment expectations and symptoms (Eells et al. 2011). It can therefore be argued that the most commonly used methods of data collection in assessment and formulation development (i.e. the clinical interview) meet these requirements.

Clinical psychology in particular places strong emphasis on elaboration upon data collected with the use of psychological theory. Indeed, Eells et al. (2011) highlight one particular difference between the psychology and psychiatry disciplines in their review of formulation literature. They assert that formulation is primarily used within psychiatry to summarise descriptive information while in psychology greater emphasis is put on integration of this data and development of hypotheses. Psychiatrists were found to be less likely than psychologists to identify potential causes, precipitants and maintaining influences of difficulty in a person's life (Eells et al. 2011).

KEY POINT

An assessment that aims to simply confirm a diagnosis may miss essential explanatory client data which may offer a more comprehensive view of client presentation, such as the presence or absence of physical activity.

A positive psychological approach to practice

It is the current authors' observation that irrespective of therapist theoretical allegiance, there seems to be a heavy problem focus in assessment and the consequent development of a formulation. Probable barriers to development of dynamic, practicable methods of assessment and formulation development have been discussed here. Perhaps a sustained effort to reach a more attainable goal of both a comprehensive and 'balanced' perspective of the lives of those with mental health difficulty could be encouraged. Until great advances in ecological research methodology permit the type of personalised science advocated for by Fisher (2015), drawing on what already established theory can offer will inform best practice in the interim.

Positive psychology is the scientific study of positive experiences and positive individual traits and the institutions that facilitate their development. A field concerned with well-being and optimal functioning, positive psychology aims to broaden the focus of clinical psychology beyond suffering and its direct alleviation. (Duckworth, Steen and Seligman 2005).

The definition of positive psychology cited above offers opportunity for parallels to be drawn with common themes evident within the sports and exercise literature previously discussed. Constructs such as well-being and optimal functioning resemble the core ideas of focus in the sports psychology literature, for example, resilience and mental toughness. A positive psychology frame offers opportunity to bridge the gap between the quest for a more balanced, dynamic consideration of an individual presenting with psychological difficulty, and the reality of the limitations posed in the context of real-world clinical practice.

KEY POINT

Positive psychology concepts of interest in sports and exercise literature such as resilience and mental toughness may be harnessed in clinical practice by empowering clients to supersede their diagnoses and focus treatment plans on future growth rather than distress alleviation.

Owens et al. (2015) provide an extensive review of research relating to the Comprehensive Model of Positive Psychological Assessment (CMPPA), originally proposed by Lopez et al. (2003; cited in Owens et al. 2015). Owens et al. (2015) outline this stepped approach to assessment and formulation development. This model is of particular appeal in the context of the current discussion, given the clear consideration for the influence of clinician negative bias and other factors akin to the influence of peripheral message cues explored by Brewer et al. (2011). These factors are emphasised within the model as having likely powerful influence on the assessing clinician's perception of an individual (and the presenting difficulty). Owens cites the pioneering work of Wright (1988) who asserted that clinicians often form negatively skewed assumptions about clients based on the salience of negative factors, for example, pathology, low mood and isolation in documentation supporting referral. Wright proposes that the perception of the assessor may be steered towards the negative to best fit the character of the available information.

A second appealing aspect of the approach supported by Owens et al. (2015), is advocacy for an acknowledgement of the inevitable lens through which the person is considered. This lens is created by clinician background, values and biases. With regard to the present working example; clinician reflection on the influence of these factors in relation to sport and exercise would support its inclusion as a topic of consideration in balanced assessment. An acceptance of the co-existence of strengths and vulnerabilities in all individuals is encouraged while the clinician sets out to develop an implicit theory of client functioning. Gathering of complementary data and testing of alternative hypotheses further combats clinician negative bias in the development of a flexible, comprehensive conceptualisation (Owens et al. 2015). The resulting formulation is one that best provides a balanced perspective of the client's strengths, resources and weaknesses and deficits.

Owens et al. (2015) provide a set of tools to support implementation of the model in clinical practice. One of these tools is the Balanced Diagnostic Impressions Model (DICE-PM). This template offers an accessible frame for application of the ideas presented in the present discussion regarding inclusion of sports and exercise data within a comprehensive, balanced formulation. The Figure 9.1 below outlines how the DICE-PM frame may support the merging of this data with clinical information to understand a person's distress in a comprehensive manner. Measures and useful interview questions to assist with operationalising the framework are outlined in Table 9.1 and Box 9.1 respectively.

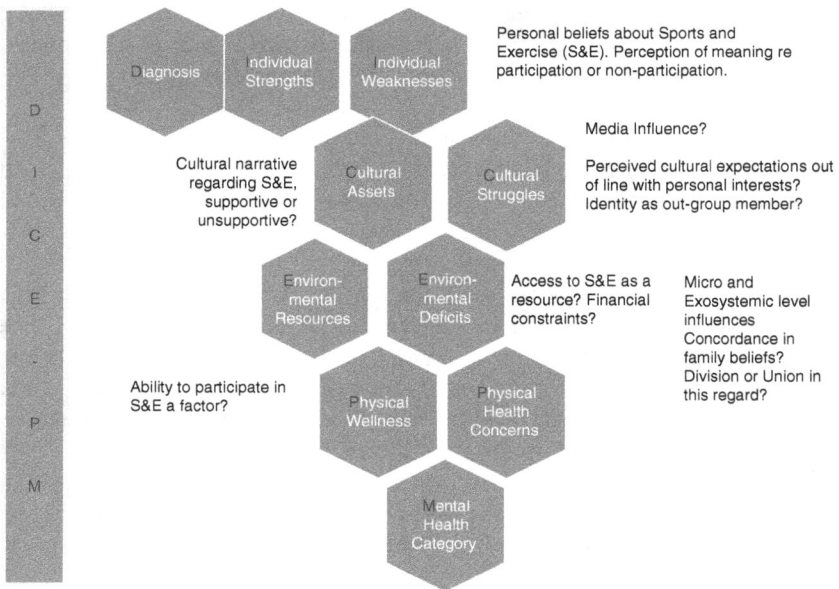

Figure 9.1 The DICE-PM model. Demonstrating potential to merge clinical and non-clinical data.

Table 9.1 Summary of available assessment tools for measuring extrinsic and intrinsic motivation in sport and exercise

Type	Sport	Exercise
Contextual measures	Sport Motivation Scale (SMS: Pelletier et al., 1995) Spon Motivation Scale-6 (SMS·6; Mallet, Kawabata, Newcombe et al., 2007) Behavioural Regulation in Sport Questionnaire (BRSQ: Lonsdale. Hodge, & Rose, 2008) Pictorial Motivation Scale (PMS; Reid, Vallerand, Poulin, Crocker, & Farrell, 2009)	Behavioural Regulation in Exercise Questionnaira (BREO: Mullan, Markland, & Ingledew, 1997) Exercise Motivation Scale (EMS; Li, 1999)
Situational measures	Situational Motivation Scale (SIMS; Guay, Vallerand, & Blanchard, 2000)	

Source: Tenenbaum, G et al. 2012. *Measurement in Sports and Exercise Psychology.* IL, USA: Human Kinetics.

BOX 9.1 SUGGESTED QUESTIONS RELATING TO SPORT AND EXERCISE FOR INCLUSION IN INTERVIEW ASSESSMENT

1. *Describe your interests and hobbies?*
   An open question to start allows the clinician to see whether the client offers spontaneous information about their participation in sport and exercise. The clinician may attune to the client's non verbal responses to the question, that is, is this question welcomed or does it elicit a defensive reaction? Does the client's response provide insight into beliefs about leisure?
2. *What do you remember learning about sport and exercise when you were a child?*
3. *Growing up, how was sport and exercise considered in your family/ school/neighbourhood/country?*
   These questions may provide the clinician with insight into any existing narrative relating to participation in sport and exercise. The questions can be phrased to target information relating to the different levels of influencing systems as per Bronfenbrenner's Ecological Systems Theory of Development (Bronfenbrenner 1979).
4. *Would you consider sport/exercise something that is important for what you stand for or want to do in life? Is it something that you would like more or less of in life?*
   This question may provide the clinician with a sense of whether the client holds important values with regard to sport and exercise. The clinician may also be able to understand whether or not the client considers themselves to be living in line with these values.

5. *What are your strengths and areas for development with regards to physical activity generally?*
6. *What things do you do that help you stay well? What have you found helps you to feel good?*

The authors of the CMPAA (Owens et al. 2015) advocate for greater balance in standard clinical intake via inclusion of open-ended questions targeting inclusive demographics, individual and environmental strengths, and areas of positive emotional experience, hope and well-being among other positive psychological constructs.

Conclusion

This chapter has focused on physical activity through the lens of sport and exercise as an area of a client's life not often considered as standard in 'standardised' assessment. The ideals set for provision of dynamic psychological assessment and formulation development for those seeking intervention for mental health difficulties have been highlighted. Having reviewed the relevant literature, and used sport and exercise as a working example of consideration of non-clinical information, an interim movement to greater application of positive psychological approaches to this task seems prudent and valid. This recommendation is set within a context of acknowledged barriers to real-world application of ideal dynamic assessment methods. Future developments may benefit from continued focus on the factors that influence clinician perception of clients and their presenting difficulties. The study of heuristics is suggested as a supportive frame of reference for this progression. Taking sport and exercise as an example of an area of clients' lives commonly considered low in clinical relevance has demonstrated how questions arising from its comprehensive consideration could provide an additional layer of data congruent with standard assessment outcomes.

REFERENCES

American Psychiatric Association. 2013. *Diagnostic and Statistical Manual of Mental Disorders*, 5th ed. Washington, DC: Author.

Beck, A.T., Ward, C., & Mendelson, M. 1961. Beck Depression Inventory (BDI). *Arch Gen Psychiatry*, 4(6), 561–571.

Brewer, N., Barnes, J., & Sauer, J. 2011. The effects of peripheral message cues on clinician's judgements about client psychological status. *British Journal of Clinical Psychology*, 50, 67–83.

British Psychological Society 2017. *Practice Guidelines*, 3rd ed. [online]. Available: https://www.bps.org.uk/sites/bps.org.uk/files/Policy/Policy%20%20Files/BPS%20Practice%20Guidelines%20(Third%20Edition).pdf

Bronfenbrenner, U. 1979. *The Ecology of Human Development: Experiments by Nature and Design.* Cambridge, MA: Harvard University Press.

Carr, A., & McNulty, M. 2011. *The Handbook of Adult Clinical Psychology: An Evidence-Based Practice Approach.* London: Routledge.

Deci, E.L. & Ryan, R.M. 1985. *Intrinsic Motivation and Self-Determination in Human Behavior.* New York: Plenum.

Division of Clinical Psychology. 2001. *The Core Purpose and Philosophy of the Profession,* Leicester: British Psychological Society.

Duckworth, A.L., Steen, T.A. & Seligman, M.E.P. 2005. Positive psychology in clinical practice. *Annual Review of Clinical Psychology,* 1, 629–51.

Eells, T.D., Lombart, K.G., Salsman, N., Kendjelic, E.M., Schneiderman, C.T., & Lucas, C.P. 2011. Expert reasoning in psychotherapy case formulation. *Journal of Psychotherapy Research,* 21(4), 385–399.

Federation of Irish Sport. 2014. *Annual Review.* Dublin IE: Author. [online]. Available: http://irishsport.ie/wpress/index.php/2014/12/federation-of-irish-sport-publish-annual-review-2014/. [August 2015].

Fisher, A.J. 2015. Toward a dynamic model of psychological assessment: Implications for personalised care. *Journal of Consulting and Clinical Psychology,* 83(4), 825–836.

Griffith, C.R. 1926. *Psychology of Coaching.* Scribner's.

Guay, F., Vallerand, R.J., & Blanchard, C. 2000. On the assessment of situational intrinsic and extrinsic motivation: The situational motivation scale (SIMS). *Motivation and Emotion,* 24, 175–213. 10.1023/A:1005614228250.

Health Professions Council 2009. *Standards of Proficiency: Practitioner Psychologists.* London: Health Professions Council.

Irish Sports Council 2013. *Irish Sports Monitor: 2013 Annual Report.* Dublin IE: Author. [online]. Available: http://www.irishsportscouncil.ie/Research/Irish-Sports-Monitor-Annual-Report-2013/ [August 2015].

Johnstone, L., & Dallos, R. 2006. *Formulation in Psychology and Psychotherapy: Making Sense of People's Problems.* Cornwall: Routledge.

Johnstone, L., & Dallos, R. 2013. *Formulation in Psychology and Psychotherapy: Making Sense of People's Problems.* Hove: Routledge.

Kern, M.L. 2016. Exercise, physical activity and mental Health. *Encyclopaedia of Mental Health,* 2, 175–180.

Li, F. 1999. The exercise motivation scale: Its multifaceted structure and construct validity. *Journal of Applied Sport Psychology,* 11:1, 97–115.

Lonsdale, C., Hodge, K., & Rose, E. A. 2008. The behavioral regulation in sport questionnaire (BRSQ): Instrument development and initial validity evidence. *Journal of Sport and Exercise Psychology,* 30(3), 323–355.

Lopez, S.J., & Snyder, C.R. (Eds.) 2003. Positive Psychological Assessment: A Handbook of Models and Measures. *American Psychological Association.*

Mallett, C., Kawabata, M., Newcombe, P., Otero-Forero, A., & Jackson, S. 2007. Sport Motivation Scale-6 (SMS-6): A revised six-factor sport motivation scale. *Psychology of Sport and Exercise.* 8. 10.1016/j.psychsport.2006.12.005.

Mullan, E., Markland, D., & Ingledew, D.K. 1997. A graded conceptualisation of self-determination in the regulation of exercise behaviour: Development of a measure using confirmatory factor analytic procedures. *Personality and Individual Differences,* 23(5), 745–752.

Owens, R.L., Magyar-Moe, J.L, & Lopez, S.J. 2015. Finding balance via positive psychological assesment and conceptualization: Implications for practice. *The Counseling Psychologist*, 1–37.

Pelletier, L.G., Tuson, K.M., Fortier, M.S., Vallerand, R.J., Briere, N.M., & Blais, M.R. 1995. Toward a new measure of intrinsic motivation, extrinsic motivation, and amotivation in sports: The Sport Motivation Scale (SMS). *Journal of Sport and Exercise Psychology*, 17(1), 35–53.

Petty, R.E., & Cacioppo, J.T. 1981. *Attitudes and Persuasion: Classic and Contemporary Approaches*. Dubuque, IA: Wm. C. Brown.

Reid, G., Vallerand, R.J., Poulin, C., & Crocker, P. 2009. The development and validation of the Pictorial Motivation Scale in physical activity. *Motivation and Emotion*, 33(2) 161–172

Sheard, M. 2013. *Mental Toughness: The Mindset Behind Sporting Achievement*, 2nd ed. Routledge: UK.

Tenenbaum, G., Eklund, R., & Kamata, A. 2012. *Measurement in Sports and Exercise Psychology*. IL, USA: Human Kinetics.

Tutko, T., Lyon, P., & Ogilvie, B. 1969. *Athletic Motivation Inventory*. San Jose, CA: Institute for the Study of Athletic Motivation.

Weinberg, R.S., & Gould, D. 2011. *Foundations of Sport and Exercise Psychology*, 5th ed. USA: Human Kinetics.

Wright, B.A. 1988. *Attitudes and fundamental negative bias: Conditions and corrections*. In H.E. Yuker (Ed.), Attitudes toward persons with disabilities (pp. 3–21). New York, NY: Springer.

Index

Note: Page number in **bold** denotes **Table**. Page number in *italics* denotes *Figure*.

cognitive functioning 55; sleep and insight 87–88; sleep, inhibition and decision making 88; sleep, memory and learning 86–87
Comprehensive Model of Positive Psychological Assessment (CMPPA) 137
confirmatory bias 23
constructivist psychology 12–13
constructivist psychotherapy 13
co-operativity 34
cosmic meaning 12
counter-transference 78–79

data 128
DBT *see* Dialectical Behaviour Therapy
declarative verbal memory, impaired 38
deconstructive questioning 21
Decreased Sexual Desire Screener (DSDS) 121; *see also* sexuality
depression 39
description, rules of 20
Diagnostic and Statistical Manual of Mental Disorders 5th Edition (DSM-V) 135
Dialectical Behaviour Therapy (DBT) 108
DICE-PM *see* Balanced Diagnostic Impressions Model
diet and nutrition 8, 51; assessment 54–56; clinical interview questions on 57–58; clinical presentations in psychological services 54–55; diet and mental health 54; formal psychometric assessment 56–57; healthy vs. unhealthy diet 53; initiating therapeutic dialogue 58–59; inventories and questionnaires 57; and mental health 52–54; Minnesota Starvation Experiment 53; open-ended questions on to 57; psychological distress reflect model 56; reflective exercise 60–61; symptomatic and non-symptomatic information 59–60
DSDS *see* Decreased Sexual Desire Screener
DSM-V *see* Diagnostic and Statistical Manual of Mental Disorders 5th Edition
Dual system model 14

eating disorders 71–72; *see also* psychological distress

Eating Identity Type Inventory (EITI) **56**
Ecological Systems theory 133
EITI *see* Eating Identity Type Inventory
Elaboration Likelihood Model 130
emotional: disorders 102; processing and sleep 88–89; recognition 36
EMS *see* Exercise Motivation Scale
epistemic meaning 12
Epsteins' Sexual Orientation Inventory (ESOI) 120; *see also* sexuality
equipotentiality 34
ESOI *see* Epsteins' Sexual Orientation Inventory
Exercise Motivation Scale (EMS) 134
existential: humanistic strategies 22; and implicit meaning 12; vacuum 13
experience cycle 12

FACIT-Sp *see* Functional Assessment of Chronic Illness Therapy–Spiritual Well-Being Scale
FAITH framework for spiritual history-taking 105–106, **106**; *see also* spirituality
Federation of Irish Sport (FIS) 131
FIS *see* Federation of Irish Sport
Five Factor Model *see* Big Five model
formulation 31; *see also* clinical formulation
freedom of will 13
Functional Assessment of Chronic Illness Therapy–Spiritual Well-Being Scale (FACIT-Sp) 104

Healthy Eating Vital Sign (HEVS) **56**
heuristic processing 130
HEVS *see* Healthy Eating Vital Sign
hippocampal system 38
hippocampus 38–39; *see also* neuroscience
horizontalization, rule of 20

identity 115
illusory correlation and representativeness biases 24
IM *see* Intrinsic Motivation
impaired declarative verbal memory 38
inattention 40
informal learning 6
insomnia 89
integrating models 58–59

Taylor & Francis Group
an **informa** business

Taylor & Francis eBooks

www.taylorfrancis.com

A single destination for eBooks from Taylor & Francis
with increased functionality and an improved user
experience to meet the needs of our customers.

90,000+ eBooks of award-winning academic content in
Humanities, Social Science, Science, Technology, Engineering,
and Medical written by a global network of editors and authors.

TAYLOR & FRANCIS EBOOKS OFFERS:

A streamlined
experience for
our library
customers

A single point
of discovery
for all of our
eBook content

Improved
search and
discovery of
content at both
book and
chapter level

REQUEST A FREE TRIAL
support@taylorfrancis.com

Routledge
Taylor & Francis Group

CRC Press
Taylor & Francis Group

For Product Safety Concerns and Information please contact our EU
representative GPSR@taylorandfrancis.com
Taylor & Francis Verlag GmbH, Kaufingerstraße 24, 80331 München, Germany

www.ingramcontent.com/pod-product-compliance
Lightning Source LLC
Chambersburg PA
CBHW052010270326
41929CB00015B/2867